Loyalties and Traditions

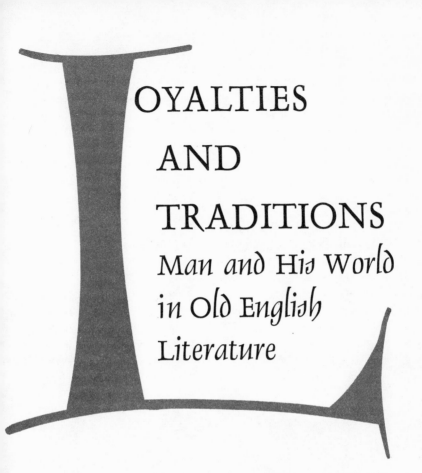

LOYALTIES AND TRADITIONS

Man and His World in Old English Literature

MILTON McC. GATCH

PEGASUS · NEW YORK   A DIVISION OF
THE BOBBS-MERRILL COMPANY, INC. *PUBLISHERS*

This book is one of a series, Pegasus Backgrounds in English Literature, under the general editorship of John R. Mulder, New York University.

for
Ione
and
George

ACKNOWLEDGMENTS

The Author and Publisher wish to thank the following for permission to reprint:

R. W. V. Elliott's translation of Cynewulf from "Cynewulf's Runes in *Christ II* and *Elene*," *English Studies*, XXXIV (1953); used by permission of Swets & Zeitlinger, Publishers, Amsterdam, The Netherlands.

From portions of the five numbered sections of the Introduction of the *Regularis Concordia*, edited and translated by Thomas Symons; used by permission of the Clarendon Press, Oxford.

Lines 558–85 of *Ascension*, translated by John C. Pope, from "The Lacuna in the Text of Cynewulf's *Ascension*," in *Studies in Language, Literature, and Culture of the Middle Ages and Later*, Atwood and Hill, editors (University of Texas Press); used by permission of John C. Pope.

From pages 92–93 of *Consolation of Philosophy*, by Boethius; used by permission of The Bobbs-Merrill Company, Inc., Indianapolis and New York.

From *Advent*, Division V, in *Poems from the Old English*, 2nd edition, translated by Burton Raffel; used by permission of the University of Nebraska Press, Lincoln, Nebraska.

From *Beowulf*, as translated by Kevin Crossley-Holland; used by permission of Farrar, Straus & Giroux, Inc., New York City.

Contents

List of Illustrations

Preface

THIS BOOK IS A STUDY OF BASIC CUSTOMS AND ASSUMPTIONS which form the backgrounds of Old English literature. It is my hope, above all, to dispel the notion that Anglo-Saxon literary culture was barbaric or primitive by stressing the sophistication, traditionalism, and learning which lie behind the writings and which give many works a poignancy and power which remain valid and effective today, nearly a millennium after the end of the Saxon era.

Necessity has rendered this study highly selective as to the subjects and Old English works discussed. I have devoted attention to topics which seem to me—and I think to most of my students—illuminating for the beginner who is ill at ease in the Early Middle Ages. In selecting texts for discussion, I have tried to achieve a balance between pieces often read by students and those usually known chiefly to specialists. I regret that it has been impossible to provide the work with full documentation. I have listed the most important works I have used in Appendix II, and I will be happy to answer readers' queries about my authorities for any point from the full set of notes in my possession.

It is a pleasure to record my thanks to a few of the many persons who have assisted me in preparing this book. Professor John C. Pope made very fruitful suggestions while the outline was being drafted. Professor Rowland L. Collins offered helpful and expert criticisms of the manuscript. Professor Robert R. Rowland, Jr., helped to check my Latin translations. Professor Edzard Baumann and Mr. Martin Biddle read and made helpful suggestions on passages dealing with art and archaeology. Professors Katherine H. Gatch and Marion W. Witt helped to edit my prose. Miss Mary Catherine Bodden generously assisted in reading the typescript. Librarians at Missouri, Harvard, and the British Museum provided invaluable assistance, and the Research Council of the University of Missouri has supported my work generously.

MILTON McC. GATCH
Columbia, Missouri, October 1970

Loyalties and Traditions

I. The Importance of Old English Literature

OLD ENGLISH LITERATURE IS UNIQUE AND IMPORTANT IN several ways. It is, in the first place, the oldest and most extensive body of European literature extant in one of the vernacular languages of the "barbarian" tribes whose migrations and settlements in the frontier areas of the Roman Empire were the final chapters of Western imperial history. The literature in Old English is not the only Germanic literature from the Early Middle Ages: there are writings in Gothic and Old High German, and two important, religious poems—the *Heliand* and the *Genesis* fragment—survive in Old Saxon; and one can assume that much more has been lost. The Anglo-Saxons, however, left the largest, most varied, and oldest body of non-Latin European literature which has survived. Much verse composed to be recited may never have been written down. Norse raiders, later ideological zealots, and the merely indifferent may have destroyed a vast part of the cultural heritage. What remains is significantly inclusive. It is the most important coherent collection of evidence about "barbarian" culture during the transition between classical and European (or modern) civilization; and it is one of the few avenues of approach to the language, culture, and beliefs of the Germanic peoples.

Furthermore, this literature is important because it represents the earliest stratum of English literary history and culture. Too often, perhaps, this assertion about Old English literature has been a feeble defense for the inclusion of Old English linguistic and literary study in the English curriculum. It *is* true that Old

English is the root and base of our language and that, after centuries of doing English grammar by analogy with Latin (a tendency which goes back to the Anglo-Saxon period), a sound knowledge of the structure of Old English has helped to sharpen our understanding of the structure of modern English. Because of its importance for historical linguistics, the teaching of the Old English language and literature has traditionally been a subsidiary task of the resident linguist in many universities. But at the present moment, when the "relevance" to their lives of any subject must be demonstrated before most students are willing to commit themselves to it, the study of Old English must renew itself through the contributions of history, theology, and literary criticism.

The relation of the literature of the Anglo-Saxons to the mainstream of English literary history is, however, tenuous. R. W. Chambers discerned certain stylistic traits of Old English prose which seemed to him to exert a continuing influence throughout the Middle Ages; and, more recently, C. L. Wrenn has suggested that there is a "limited" continuity in the poetic technique and that the didactic and elegiac tendencies of Old English verse have persisted into the modern period. Whether or not these arguments are cogent, the beginning student of Old English may well feel that the stylistic continuities are fortuitous and the thematic ones entangled in the human condition. English prose has lent itself to rhetorical decoration and balance so that the prose of Ælfric looks similar to that of the authors of early Middle English religious prose. Poets of the Middle English period of such varied temperaments as Layamon and the authors of *Sir Gawain and the Green Knight* and *Piers Plowman* obviously harked back to Old English poetic structural principles, chiefly alliteration. Moralism and melancholy mark serious English poetry not only through the Middle Ages but also into the work of such poets as T. S. Eliot. If the student is more impressed by dissimilarity than by similarity, he can fall back on the fact that the Norman Conquest of England coincided with (and, indeed, was part of) a major and international cultural revolution which so altered all of European culture that what followed can justly be said to be the product of a different civilization.

Literary historians have often blurred the distinctions between the Dark or Early Middle Ages and the Later or High Middle Ages. It is necessary, first of all, to stress the fact that the Roman Empire did not fall but rather, for a combination of reasons ranging from trends in agricultural economy to intellectual movements, withered away in a manner which those who were alive at the time did not fully comprehend. While a number of Romans saw that cultural standards had been diluted by contact with the barbarians and by internal compromises, many of the barbarian settlers in the Empire imagined that they had become full members of the Roman cultural and political system. The late Henri Pirenne argued that the Roman Empire, a cosmopolitan community based on free interchange across the Mediterranean, continued to exist (however decayed its cultural and economic institutions) until the Arab invasions of the seventh and eighth centuries. The Arab conquest, Pirenne believed, turned the Mediterranean into a "Muslim lake" and forced the Christian West to turn in upon itself. The "Pirenne thesis" was based primarily upon the evidence of economic history and has generally been discredited on those very grounds. The Arab invasions did not cause the demise of the Roman system of a trade-based, urban economy, for economic decay had already proceeded farther than Pirenne was willing to admit. His theory was, however, responsible for a reassessment of early medieval history and of the fall of Rome, and it is now generally conceded that the Empire passed away almost unnoticed and that the barbarians, far from wanting to destroy the civilization with which they came in contact, wanted to absorb its culture and other benefits. The barbarian kingdoms, notably that of the Carolingians, regarded themselves as continuous with the Roman civil order; classical culture was kept alive and disseminated by the Christian scholars; and the idea of the primacy of Rome's bishop over the church was maintained, especially by the Anglo-Saxons, throughout a period during which the popes themselves were too weak and dissipated to assert it.

The society and culture of the Early Middle Ages, then, was classical—although classical in a very special form. Men were aware that theirs was a debased culture, but they had no sense of having inaugurated a new order or built a new civilization. They wanted only to preserve what was left of the old: the learning of the classical world; Christianity, the official religion of the later imperial period; and, in the Carolingian and Anglo-Saxon kingdoms, something of the sense of a lawfully ordered body politic. The unique characteristics of this post-Roman Latin culture, modified by the absorption and conversion of the barbarian Germans, are the subject of the chapters which are to follow. It was different from the classical civilization of the Roman Empire, but for the moment it is more important to stress continuity if we are to come to an understanding of the meaning and historical importance of the Anglo-Saxon period or of the Early Middle Ages in general.

The end of the age just described coincided with the Norman Conquest of England in 1066. The very settlement of the Normans in England and in Sicily represented the end of the long period of Germanic migration, invasion, and assimilation. This demographic stabilization coincided with a fresh burst of energy throughout Europe of which a growth of population and the revival of urban life and trade were important factors. Most important, however, was the revolution in intellectual life, which was stimulated at every turn by the revival of the discipline of logic—or dialectics. Dialectics had always been part of the trivium of the late classical educational curriculum, but it had been almost totally neglected in the Early Middle Ages when grammar and rhetoric or even grammar alone had seemed to suffice for a liberal education. For the High Middle Ages, dialectics was the primary intellectual discipline by which man analyzed and organized his knowledge for the purpose of solving problems and organizing his life. Logic was not responsible for the new, highly articulated social structure which characterized the period, but it was of the same spirit and was brought to bear on the elaborately articulated rationale for the new, hierarchical, military-based system of land tenure which we call feudalism. The burst of educational activity, in which logic was the tool used to organize all fields of knowledge from medicine and law to theology, also called forth a whole new system of higher education. The eleventh century, in other words, saw the birth of a new civilization—of Europe—in a remarkable burst of physical, economic, and intellectual energy.

The end of the Anglo-Saxon age and the coming of the Normans coincided with this cultural revolution. Thus it is that the student who is as impressed with the discontinuity between the literatures of the Old and the Middle English periods as with their continuity is basically correct in his feeling. Were other early medieval vernacular literatures extant, it is very likely that they would provide evidence for the same kinds of radical change. Certainly Latin literature—the chief surviving vehicle of medieval intellectual activity—testifies to the change. To take but one example, theology in the earlier period contented itself with the reproduction of the wisdom of the Fathers of the Church. When it considered the manner in which Christ effected the salvation of mankind, it looked to Christ's descent into hell ("the harrowing of hell") and imagined that he overcame Satan by tricking him, just as Satan had tricked Adam. In the twelfth century, Anselm (who was, among other things, a Norman archbishop of Canterbury) argued that this explanation of salvation was illogical and, therefore, beneath God's dignity. Highly conscious of being an innovator, he developed a logical explanation of the reasons for and method of atonement based upon the axiom that God is, above all, just. The feudal and legal ideas of strict but compassionate justice thus provided him with the model for a new, more legal, and more human theory of atonement.

The case cited is but one among many. Wherever one turns, the evidence suggests that a cultural revolution occurred in Europe in the eleventh century and that the upheaval coincided with the boundaries between the Saxon and Norman periods in England. Old English literature is thus significantly different from or discontinuous with Middle English literature not because of the introduction of Latinate or romance words, literary forms, and ideas, but because all of Western Europe underwent a radical change at the same time.

If this is true, the task of the teacher of Old English in justifying the importance of his specialization to his students is, at least superficially, more difficult. One need not necessarily know *Beowulf* or the writings of King Alfred in order to understand the works of the alliterative revival of the fourteenth century. The study of the one contributes to the appreciation of the other chiefly insofar as it sharpens the reader's awareness of the differences between the two. The historical importance of Old English writing rests on the fact that it is the unique evidence of the literary and intellectual culture of a converted Germanic people on the frontier of the old Empire, where the adoption of Latin as the lingua franca was either not possible or not desirable, during the period of transition between classical and European civilization. English is simply the only language in which extensive evidence for this period survives, and the study of English language and literature is invaluable for cultural historians.

The twentieth century is itself a period of radical change. However little we are able to imagine what is emerging in our world, we can perceive that change and the tensions of transition are basic facts of our existence. An understanding of what the experience of a transitional culture meant to the Anglo-Saxons may be important to us both as an example and as a source of comfort and courage. Several aspects of the Old English poetry are notably congenial in the late twentieth century. The first is that much of the verse of the Anglo-Saxons deals with violence. The irrational and hostile forces with which man found himself confronted—even as we are confronted—evoked in the best poetry an attitude of perseverance in the pursuit of one's ideals in spite of the possibility, or even probability, of defeat. The typical Anglo-Saxon attitude is not unlike that stated by Albert Camus in his novel, *The Plague,* written in the aftermath of World War II:

> Dr. Rieux resolved to compile this chronicle, so that he should not be one of those who hold their peace but should bear witness in favor of those plague-stricken people; so that some memorial of the injustice and outrage done them might endure; and to state quite simply what we learn in a time of pestilence: that there are more things to admire in men than to despise.

Second, much Old English poetry conveys a sense of alienation not dissimilar to that in much modern literature. Man, the elegists declare, is alone and cruelly buffeted by fate and nature. If many of us (like Ezra Pound in his translation of *The Seafarer*) cannot follow the Old English poets to their conclusion that the way out of alienation is through a relationship with the Christian God, we are at least able to share their sense of the futility of life in this world. Finally, and closely related to the theme of alienation, is the notion that the earth, like man, ages and decays and is now in its dotage. The theme arises in Old English from a classical tradition which looks nostalgically to a "golden" age; and although it has not generally been regarded as one of the most poignant motifs, it may come to strike a more sympathetic chord as our new understanding of the threat to life itself caused by man's destruction of his environment leads us to a sense of the past beauty and health of nature in an age now gone.

These aspects of Old English literature, which arise from the historical circumstances of its creation but which are still fresh and effective, point to the chief reason it is still studied: Old English literature is valuable, above all, because much of it is good literature. The greatness of the writings has, however, been obscured for many readers by the linguistic problem, by the resistance of these pieces to the labors of the translator, and —most important—by the cultural differences which stand between the contemporary reader and the original reader or hearer. It is, of course, possible to read *Beowulf* in very able translations with a sense of its power, its rich and complicated fabric, and its portrayal of a remarkable hero against the background of an existence which is unstable and ambiguous. It is possible, as several critics have recently demonstrated, to study analytically the texts as they have been received and to come to a more exact understanding of the skill of the weavers of the words. But only against an understanding of the writers' cultural backgrounds—those assumptions and methods which are so much a part of the writers that they tend to be implicit and not explicit —can one come to a full appreciation of their achievements.

It is the purpose of this book to explore some of the major backgrounds of Old English literature, starting wherever possible from some real problem of explication of the literary texts. No pretense is made that all the problems are covered in this study, but it is hoped that sufficient background will be provided for most readers and that adequate suggestions will be given to those who wish to pursue some of these issues further or to open others.

One of the difficulties of a book on the backgrounds of Old English literature is that, although the surviving corpus (especially of poetry) is fairly small, the chronological period covered is quite long. The Anglo-Saxon penetration of England began in the fifth century. In the last decade of the sixth century, Pope

Gregory the Great sent missionaries to Kent. These missionaries and their successors (with the aid—or as they sometimes saw it, interference—of Irish monks) undertook the work of conversion. With this confrontation of the Germanic settlers of Britain and classical, Christian culture, Anglo-Saxon history begins. The seventh century saw a remarkable cultural flowering, a "Northumbrian Renaissance," of which Bede is only the greatest literary figure; and during the following century Anglo-Saxon monks did important missionary work on the Continent. But a period of troubles caused by the raids of pirates from the North began in the eighth century; Northumbrian culture was destroyed and the southern Anglo-Saxon kingdoms were sorely threatened. Resistance was led by the kings of the West Saxons, notably Alfred (d. 900), who not only reestablished a measure of order but also carried out military, social, and educational reforms. Alfred's successors, aided especially by monastic reformers in the tenth century, made of a loose hegemony of independent monarchies (the "Heptarchy") a fairly strong and unified England with a high level of culture which survived, despite continued difficulties with the Northmen and a final dynastic debacle, until the Conquest of 1066. Indeed, William's conquest was based on a fairly plausible claim to the throne and, were it not for the cultural transformations with which it coincided, might not have seemed as decisive an event as it has been considered.

The five centuries of Anglo-Saxon history, so sketchily summarized in the preceding paragraph, make an unwieldy era for one who wants to treat literary backgrounds. But although they were not uneventful years, and although the kinds of assumptions brought to the literature by writers and readers were themselves subject to change during the period of Old English literary activity, there is nevertheless a general homogeneity of attitude. For our present purposes it seems advisable, therefore, to avoid such vexing issues as the nature and extent of Irish influence and of pagan survivals in the seventh through the ninth centuries in order to concentrate on a part of the Saxon era, the period from Alfred to the Conquest. Without ignoring documents of the seventh, eighth, and ninth centuries, I have arbitrarily explored the century 900–1020, focusing on the backgrounds or attitudes of the literary audience of that period.

Several factors make this approach defensible and even desirable. For one thing, Old English poetry survives in manuscripts which can almost all be dated around the year 1000, and the earliest prose of any literary value is from the reign of Alfred. Thus, although some Old English poetry and prose originated in earlier periods, it is only reasonable to consider the literature in the light of the age in which it was preserved.

The decision to view the literature from the point of view of the late-Saxon period underscores the extremely important point that Anglo-Saxon culture was a Christian culture. The little we know about the pagan, Germanic backgrounds of Old English literature was transmitted to us by Christian Anglo-Saxons and must therefore be carefully interpreted. The very writing of the language, the recording of poetry, the transcription of legal codes and documents were undertaken as a result of the meeting of the Anglo-Saxons with Latin Christianity. Most recent students of Old English literature have found it far easier to document the dependence of the writers on the commonplaces of the Latin, Christian tradition than to trace their roots in the Germanic world. Thus, even though this book begins with a discussion of Germanic backgrounds, that approach must be regarded as highly artificial, since it is impossible to isolate the purely Germanic (or for that matter the purely Christian) in the literature of the Anglo-Saxons.

This book is not written on a chronological continuum and is only peripherally concerned with development. It moves, rather, topically, treating in succession a number of subjects which (it seems to me) must be understood if one is to appreciate the Old English literature as literature produced within and for the members of early medieval society. Earlier studies of literary backgrounds have been largely concerned with scientific presuppositions and have often been restricted even more to cosmology or the received understanding of the nature and composition of the universe. A number of later background studies have also considered education in order to clarify the kinds of training and the intellectual habits and customs which a writer brought to his work. These considerations both figure in this book, but, although it would be possible and valuable to study at much greater length Anglo-Saxon cosmological views and education, it has seemed to me as important to attempt to outline as well a number of social attitudes which made the lives of the Anglo-Saxons different from those of later medieval men and from our own. If I were to define "literary backgrounds," then, the term would have to comprehend as many as possible of the conditions and attitudes which make the life and intellect (and, therefore, the literary productions) of a given age different from those of other ages. It is my hope that this study deals more or less adequately with most of the conditions and attitudes which made the tenth- or eleventh-century reader different from the twentieth-century reader of Old English and that it will help the modern reader to enter the mind of the reader or hearer for whose edification and pleasure the Anglo-Saxon writers worked.

II. The Germanic Backgrounds

ONLY TWO ASSERTIONS ABOUT THE PERSEVERANCE OF CUS-TOMS from the Germanic past of the Anglo-Saxons can be made with very great confidence. The first is that it was somehow important for the Anglo-Saxons even as late as the tenth and eleventh centuries to maintain a Germanic identity by reminding themselves of their ancestry. The second is that throughout the Old English period they continued to make poetry in a manner derived from the Germanic tradition of prosody. Only after one has examined these two assertions, can he raise the question of what other factors remained in the customs and assumptions of the Anglo-Saxons from their pre-Christian past.

A. THE RACIAL MEMORY.

Weland experienced persecution by hindrances, the strong-minded man underwent hardships; he had sorrow and longing as his companion, winter-cold misery; often he came to know woe after Nithhad laid fetters, supple sinew-bonds, on him, the better man.
  That passed; so can this.

For Beaduhild, her brother's death was not so grievous as her own trouble: she clearly perceived that she was pregnant; she was unable ever to consider resolutely, how she ought to act about it.
  That passed; so can this.

We heard that the moans of Mæthhild, Geat's lady, were boundless, so that the sorrowful love deprived her of all sleep.
  That passed; so can this.

Theodoric ruled the town of the Mærings for thirty winters; it
was known to many.

    That passed; so can this.

We learned by asking of the wolfish thought of Eormanric; he
had wide sway over the people of the Gothic kingdom; that was a
savage king. Many a man sat bound by sorrows, in expectations
of woe and wished frequently that the kingdom would be over-
thrown.

    That passed; so can this.

If a man sits, sorrowful and deprived of joys, he becomes gloomy
in mind, it seems to him as though his portion of tribulations
were endless; then he can consider that throughout the world
the wise Lord frequently changes; to many a man he shows mercy,
certainty of joys; to others a share of woe.

About myself I want to say that I was for a time the scop of the
people of Heden, dear to the lord; my name was Deor. For many
winters I had a good office, a gracious lord—until now Heorrenda,
a man skilled in song, received the land which the protector of
men had formerly granted to me.

    That passed; so can this.

Deor, the poem printed above, bristles with difficulties. The
text in the Exeter Book contains a number of puzzling readings.
Its semi-stanzaic form and use of something like a refrain are
(except for the even more difficult *Wulf and Eadwacer* and
the *Seasons for Fasting*) unique in Old English. Its allusions to
Germanic legend and myth are so oblique that it is difficult to
know just what point the poet wants to make and whether he
has succeeded. It purports, at the end, to have been written in
the heroic age, but it has apparent references to the Christian
God. It is for the most part based on specific allusions to the
Germanic past, but lines 28–34 change startlingly and (some have
felt) incongruously from the specific to the general. Although the
use of a fictional persona is a chief device of the Old English
elegy, the unusually concrete *Deor*-persona is, as Frederick Norman has remarked, "one of the freshest and most original con-
ceits in Old English poetry." The poem cannot be dated with

accuracy, although the late ninth century—or, roughly, the time of Alfred the Great—strikes a recent editor as possible.

It is, however, generally presumed that the author of *Deor* was a Christian; and, whether or not he was writing in the elegiac tradition, as the refrain seems to indicate, he was making an observation about the transitoriness of the suffering of unfortunate men. The point is an unusual one: the more frequent sort of thing in the elegiac tradition would be to discuss the transitoriness of prosperity and pleasure; but the negative position is a necessary corollary of the positive.

What is most obvious about the poem is also most remarkable: that to make his point the Christian poet draws examples from the heroic or Germanic world. Whether the poet wrote in the eighth century or the tenth, one might not expect this kind of example. Alcuin, who was trained during the Northumbrian renaissance and helped to inaugurate the Carolingian renaissance, had written to the monks of Lindisfarne after the first raids of the Northmen in the last decade of the eighth century to suggest that the disaster they had suffered was not without historical parallel in the experiences of Jerusalem and Rome. Having hinted in the same letter that the monks indulged in drunken banquets, he charged more forthrightly in a later letter that the harpist usurped the place of the lector or reader of works of Christian edification at monastic meals and that the monks delighted more in Germanic tales than in the word of God. "Quid Hinieldus cum Christo?"—"What has Ingeld to do with Christ?"—he had thundered, consciously imitating the famous outburst of Tertullian (c. 200), "What indeed has Athens to do with Jerusalem?" The implication is, of course, that even the religious in the great century of Northumbrian monastic culture cared more for secular, pagan reminiscence than for Christian learning. Gregory the Great had advised his missionaries to Kent not to destroy the pagan places of worship but to destroy the idols and reconsecrate sanctuaries to Christian use. However, given the tensions—not only between Christian and pagan but also between Latin and Celtic Christians—it was inevitable that difficulties would arise and efforts be made to refute and to eradicate the memory of the pagan past.

Pagan and Germanic place-names in England provided very important evidence for the history and progress of the Anglo-Saxon settlement, but the place-names give us little information about the heroes and deities commemorated because the associations of the names have been lost or suppressed. In the first half of the eighth century, the great historian Bede appears to have been almost totally ignorant of the deities and teaching of Anglo-Saxon paganism. At the end of the Saxon period, Ælfric devoted a long homily to the refutation of paganism in the light of the Danish invasions; but he does not go beyond a rudimentary identification of some of the members of the Roman pantheon with their Danish counterparts; and, according to Ælfric's editor, "What he has written is much more a reassuring celebration of God's triumph over a series of foolish pretenders than a frontal assault on contemporary evils." The memory of the content of Germanic paganism was, in other words, all but eradicated so that it has become, in the words of E. G. Stanley, an "unknowable unknown."

Despite the near-eradication of Germanic religious mythology and of the religious content of Germanic legend, however, the Anglo-Saxons retained tales from the Germanic past and a lively sense of the fact that, ethnically, their identity was Germanic. *Deor* is but one of a number of striking examples of this persistence.

Another important kind of evidence for the perseverance of a sense of Germanic identity is a group of West-Saxon genealogies in the *Anglo-Saxon Chronicle* which purport to trace the ancestry of the West Saxon kings. One of these, which is part of a preface of the "A" or "Parker" version of the *Chronicle*, begins by looking back from the fifth-century settlements:

> In the year when 494 years had passed from Christ's birth, Cerdic and his son Cynric landed at *Cerdicesora* with five ships; and Cerdic was the son of Elesa, the son of Esla, the son of Gewis, the son of Wig, the son of Freawine, the son of Frithugar, the son of Brand, the son of Bældæg, the son of Woden.

From this point the account traces the succession from Cerdic through the ninth century, insisting at frequent intervals that all the West-Saxon leaders had descended from Cerdic. The first backward-looking sentence is interesting, however, for its concern to place the West-Saxon royal family's history securely within two contexts: that of Christian history and that of Germanic legend. The same kings who associated their destiny with the Christian scheme of salvation and its chronology traced their genealogy to an important figure in the pantheon of Germanic deities. It is known from the survival of Woden's name as an element of place-names and from almost all the royal genealogies of the Anglo-Saxon settlers of England that his cult had been widespread. It is likely that Woden was regarded as the common progenitor of the Germanic peoples, and it is a permissible further supposition that the continued recognition of Woden's role in the genealogies of Christian kings was an important element in the self-identification and self-understanding of their people. As late as the eleventh century, Ælfric identified Woden (using a variant of the Norse form of the name, Oðon) as Mercury, a man deified by the heathens. But Ælfric avoids elaborating on his knowledge (if any) of Woden's life and acts, and he does not mention his connection with the genealogies. Similarly, the genealogies avoid by silence the embarrassing possible implications of the divinity of this progenitor of kings. It is enough that Alfred and his house are descended from a line of which any Germanic chieftain in the Continental homeland or abroad would have been proud.

The *Chronicle* genealogies may be themselves an innovation of the reign of Alfred, however. Since Bede alludes to the custom of tracing the descent of the Northumbrian kings from Woden, this tradition must be very ancient and virtually universal in the Germanic kingdoms. But there is little evidence in the earlier period of Germanic history of a tradition of long genealogies. An account of the preceding three or four generations apparently sufficed to establish the legitimacy of a reigning king. It has been argued very cogently that the genealogies were put together over a period of time and that the more remote sections—especially those concerned with the period before the Saxon settlement in England—are actually the most recent in time of composition and, therefore, the least trustworthy as historical documentation. The evidence seems to point to Offa of Mercia in the latter half of the eighth century as an originator of the more elaborate genealogies, and his concern with legitimacy may have been influenced by the similar preoccupations of Charlemagne. Alfred, under whom the genealogical concern reached its fullest flowering, was the scion of the last surviving Anglo-Saxon royal line. It is possible that the very idea for the most highly articulated genealogical lists came from biblical genealogies, for the one entered in the *Chronicle* under 855 traces the West-Saxon ancestry to Adam through a mythological forebear "who was born in Noah's ark." Whatever the case may have been, the interest in elaborate genealogies was a comparatively late, antiquarian exercise which testifies to an unusual effort to keep alive the Germanic identity of the Christian Anglo-Saxons and to understand that ethnic heritage within a biblical framework.

Beowulf provides more inferential evidence of the high value placed by Englishmen on their Germanic heritage. It is, in the first place, a story wrought in Christian England but concerning a hero whose life is set against the background of events and peoples in northern Europe in the sixth century: Hrothgar and his hall, Heorot, were widely celebrated; the defeat of Hygelac by Theodoric is recorded by Gregory of Tours in the *History of the Franks*. But perhaps even more interesting are the implications of the arguments of Professor Dorothy Whitelock, who has shown that the social background of *Beowulf* presupposes not a pagan Germanic audience but English society in the Saxon period. Thus, one assumes, the picture of courts which delight in the recitation of tales based on the earlier exploits of North-European barbarian peoples reflects not only the supposed entertainment of Germanic warriors at leisure but also the social pastimes of the audience for whom *Beowulf* was sung as it is now recorded. If there is no corroborative evidence from the eighth century when *Beowulf* was presumably composed, there is at least the evidence in Asser's *Life of King Alfred* that the great ninth-century West-Saxon king delighted in Saxon poetry, some of which, one assumes, recounted heroic exploits. That *Beowulf,* along with poems like *Deor* and *Widsith,* was recopied at the end of the tenth century testifies to the continuing appeal of the Germanic past to the Christian Anglo-Saxons. In the case of *Beowulf,* it has recently been suggested that renewed contact with heathen cousins on the Continent through the Anglo-Saxon missionaries may account for a revival of interest in and sympathy for the pagan past.

The evidence in the works of Ælfric and Wulfstan in the eleventh century (it must be remembered that the surviving copies of the poems are about contemporary with the writings of the great homilists) is that there was no widespread anti-pagan revulsion as a result of the long period of Viking raids. Whatever the case may have been, there is recent archaeological evidence that on the eve of the Conquest reference was made to Germanic legend in order to stress the similarity of the ethnic origins of the Scandinavian raiders and their victims. In 1965, archaeologists working in the cathedral precincts at Winchester discovered a fragment of a frieze sculpture which had been destroyed in 1093–94 when the Old Minster was demolished to make way for the new Norman cathedral (Plate 1). The fragment apparently is part of two scenes of a long, narrative frieze. It is composed in a manner not unlike that of the Bayeux tapestry, which commemorates the victory of 1066; and this stylistic likeness to the tapestry suggests that the frieze must have been made in the eleventh century, not long before the Norman Conquest. In the scene to the left, a figure wearing a chain-mail shirt and a sword is walking away. The scene to the right shows a man on his back, his hand and neck bound to the ground; a dog or wolf atop the man has her paw on the chin and her tongue in the mouth of the captive. It has been suggested that the story depicted in the frieze fragment is an incident from the adventures of Sigmund which is related in the *Volsunga Saga*. The hero and his nine brothers, it is said, were bound in stocks. Nightly a wolf appeared and devoured one of the ten until only Sigmund was left. His sister, Signy, had his face smeared with honey and some of the sweet food was also put in his mouth. When the wolf appeared again, she licked the honey from his face and put her tongue into his mouth to get the rest. Sigmund seized the tongue with his teeth and, after a struggle, tore it out, thus killing his enemy and gaining his own freedom. If this is the story depicted by the frieze sculpture from the Old Minster, it testifies to continued interest in Germanic legend at a very late period and at a center which fostered both the revival of monasticism and considerable activity in the arts connected with bookmaking. If the carving was, as the archaeologist who discovered it has claimed, part of a long,

PLATE 1.
 Sigmund and the Wolf (?).

narrative sculpture which decorated the Minster where the West-Saxon kings were buried, it argues strongly for the continued interest of the Christian kings in their legendary pagan forebears. And, if the piece can be even more positively dated to the reign of Cnut, the great Scandinavian king of the English who died in 1035 and was buried at the Old Minster in Winchester, it may have been part of an effort by the foreign, but Germanic, king to stress the common ancestry of his people and those over whom he ruled. At any rate, allowing always for the possibility that the subject of the relief may not have been correctly identified, the carving from the Old Minster suggests strongly that, near the end of the Saxon period, scenes from Germanic legend formed a part of the decorative schema of the church complex most closely associated with the kings of the Anglo-Saxons. Apart from the anthology of poetry in the great Exeter Book, it had generally been thought that such mingling of Christian with pagan motifs had been a much earlier phenomenon, a feature of the seventh- and eighth-century age of *Beowulf* and Sutton Hoo and the Franks Casket.

If one turns back to *Deor* from the examination of these varied evidences of continued English Christian interest in the Germanic past, the poem's mixture of motifs becomes not less remarkable but perhaps more comprehensible. In the cases of the genealogies and the Old Minster carving, the racial memory is evoked in order to undergird both the claims of rulers to legitimacy and their understanding of their place in history. In the case of *Beowulf*, the past is recalled for purposes of entertainment and edification. *Deor*, by the device of the persona or fictitious narrator who suffered changing fortune, calls upon Germanic legend for examples of the universality of ill fortune and of the fact that, man being mortal, his life of suffering must pass. Whether one sees the poem, with Bloomfield, as a charm against evil fortune or, with Greenfield, as "over-ridingly elegiac," it is the presumably Christian poet's exempla which remain the most unusual feature of the poem to the modern reader and, given the pride of the Anglo-Saxons in their ethnic heritage, its most typically Old English trait.

Indeed, it might be argued that one of the primary facts of life in Northern Europe in the Early Middle Ages, although it began in the Roman period in the age of Caesar, was the kind of cultural dislocation which accompanies mobility. In this case, the mobility and dislocation were not the kind of voluntary social, religious, and geographical freedom which have become a fact of life and chief source of anxiety for twentieth-century man, but the sort of mobility and dislocation which is attendant upon an age of migration—the mobility and dislocation of peoples or groups, not of individuals. Thus, if it has a modern analogue, it is with the experiences of the European settlers in America in the nineteenth century, with their efforts to maintain some semblance of their national and ethnic identities, and with their frequent sense of alienation and anxiety.

The reasons for Germanic migration are lost, although they seem to have included population pressures, poverty, and sometimes avarice, and even the attractiveness of classical civilization. Although the Anglo-Saxons were a settled people by the time of their conversion in the seventh century, they never forgot that their fathers had come across the water and they were almost compulsive in their attempts to keep alive some memory of their heritage. They forgot much that we should like to know, particularly the nature and content of their pre-Christian religion, but they remembered and often tried to emulate an age of heroes who fought courageously against the outrages of fate or fortune. And despite centuries of harrassment by their Scandinavian cousins, who were part of the next wave of the migrations and who threatened the Saxons with the same fate they had meted to those whom they had displaced in Britain, they seem never to have seriously contemplated an effort to root out the memory of their common, heroic, pagan past.

B. Poetry as the Medium of Memory

The Anglo-Saxons preserved their ethnic memories and also communicated newer reflections upon man's lot in the world by means of poetry made in a manner which they had learned before coming to Britain. Oral literature and the Germanic tradition of prosody are difficult to comprehend in a society like ours which depends upon writing as a crutch for memory and which has constructed intricate tools for the retrieval of information. Perhaps, however, a poem related to *Deor* in its use of a fictitious poet as narrator and in its reliance on Germanic traditions will help to introduce these subjects:

> WIDSITH spoke, unlocked his word-hoard, he who of men had fared through most races and peoples over the earth; often he had received in hall precious treasure. His ancestors sprang from the Myrgings. He with Ealhhild, gracious weaver of peace, first, from Angel in the east, sought the home of the Gothic king Eormanric, the savage faithless one. He began then to speak many things:

> "I have heard of many men ruling over the peoples; every prince must needs live fittingly; one earl after another must rule the land, he who wishes his throne to prosper. . . . Ætla ruled the Huns, Eormanric the Goths, Becca the Banings, Gifica the Burgundians. Cæsar ruled the Greeks and Cælic the Finns, Hagena the Island-Rugians and Heoden the Glommas. . . . Offa ruled Angel, Alewih the Danes: he was bravest of all these men, yet he did not perform mighty deeds beyond Offa; but Offa, first of men, while still a youth, gained the greatest of kingdoms; no one of the same age achieved greater deeds of valour in battle: with his single sword he fixed the boundary against the Myrgings at Fifeldor. Afterwards the Angles and Swabians held it as Offa had won it. Hrothwulf and Hrothgar kept peace for a very long time, uncle and nephew, when they had driven away the race of the Vikings and overcome the array of Ingeld, destroyed at Heorot the host of the Heathobards. Thus I travelled through many foreign lands, through this wide world; good and evil I suffered there, cut off from kinsmen, far from those of my blood; I served far and wide.

> "Wherefore I may sing and utter a measure; recite before the company in the mead hall how the noble ones were liberal to me in their generosity. I was with the Huns and with the glorious Goths, with the Swedes and with Geats and with South-Danes. . . ."
>
> (lines 1–13, 18–21, 35–58)

Widsith, the poem translated above, is one of the oldest Old English poems. It was, however, copied into the Exeter Book in the period selected as the focus for this book, and it is as a relatively ancient work known to the late Anglo-Saxon reading public that it is under consideration here.

Like *Deor*, *Widsith* is based on the conceit of an imaginary *scop* or singer of tales. Unlike *Deor*, however, the conceit is not a device for reflecting upon experience (that of mankind in general) but for giving an impression of the scope and grandeur of the Germanic heroic age. The elegiac motif of separation from friends and kinsmen is alluded to in lines 50–53, but the theme of hardship is hardly central to *Widsith* as it is to *Deor*. Rather, three lists of the names of ancient heroes and their peoples are put together by means of the device of the far-travelling gleeman or minstrel so as to evoke a sense of the age of heroes from the third through the eighth centuries. The three name-lists or *thulas* of *Widsith* are generally regarded as ancient, though they differ in form. The first lists kings and their tribes (*x* ruled *y*); at the end the poet expands upon Offa and Hrothgar. The second thula follows the formula, "I was with the . . . ," and invokes the names of Germanic tribes. (The inclusion of biblical peoples in lines 82–83 has been a stumbling block for students of the poem. In effect it is, like the allusions to biblical patriarchs in the genealogies, an effort to see legendary Germanic events on a universal plane.) The final thula is based on the formula, "I sought . . . ," and lists a number of heroes, mixing both historical and fictitious figures.

Widsith is of interest here because of the hints it gives us about the craft and function of Germanic poetry. First, there is the fact that it incorporates thulas which probably were not originally composed by the author of *Widsith* but were traditional and captured the attention of a poet with antiquarian interests. Like the genealogical lists of the *Chronicle,* they seem to testify to a need to keep some basic historical facts available in easily memorizable form. Second, the very device of the fictitious poet whose Methuselan longevity gives authority to what he says, calls to mind the multiple function of the singer of tales in Germanic society as historian and bearer of wisdom as well as entertainer. The formula with which the poet introduces Widsith's speech suggests these functions:

> Widsið maðolade, wordhord onleac
> (Widsith spoke, unlocked his word-hoard).

Widsith speaks not from personal experience or in his individual voice but from and within his tradition. The treasury of words he opened contained traditional language, formulas, and themes.

When the Anglo-Saxon poet looked back to his Germanic

poetic heritage, he looked to a society which depended upon oral retention as the means of preservation and transmission of its traditions. In such a society the role of persons trained in the discipline of recitation transcended mere entertainment. History, legend, wisdom, and law were probably among the contents of his storehouse, and his functions at least impinged upon the priestly and judicial. The accuracy with which he passed on these cultural legacies was, therefore, extremely important. It is known that remarkably accurate retention was a characteristic of oral singers in societies as widely different as Hebraic, Germanic, and early Greek, and (in modern times) the Muslim Guslars in Yugoslavia. Yet, at least in the case of tales sung for entertainment, the act of singing was an act of creation: each telling of a tale was a fresh composition.

The method the singer used in performing his task can be spelled out by reference to three closely related subtopics, each of which can be documented by reference to *Widsith:* the use of formulas and other mnemonic devices, the prosody of Germanic poetry, and the use of accompaniment. Each of these areas poses difficulties for the scholar, and in the discussion which follows, it is not possible to consider any of the problems in detail. Rather, the effort has been to present a simplified and sometimes conjectural picture of the process of oral composition in Germanic society based on scholarly reconstructions and analogies. Whether these same methods prevailed in the Anglo-Saxon period itself is another question to be considered later.

1. Formulaic diction.

Expressions like *wordhord onleac*, especially if it is interpreted as related to the famous *word oþer fand/soðe gebunden* ("he found other words, fitly joined," *Beowulf*, lines 870b–871a), suggest that the poet had more in his hoard than a vocabulary of individual words. He had, it is generally agreed, a stock of groups of words or formulas upon which he could call without pausing in the process of simultaneous composition and recitation. The process of development of the formulaic word-hoard was presumably a long one which involved the community of poets over many generations. A formula was doubtless "invented" by a given poet;

it was then presumably imitated by others and tested over a period of time for aesthetic quality and for usefulness; subsequently it was either dropped or made a part of the community's collection of stock phrases. Professor Milman Parry described the use of the communal hoard of formulas:

> In time the needed number of such phrases is made up: each idea to be expressed in the poetry has its formula for each metrical need, and the poet, who would not think of trying to express ideas outside the traditional field of thought of poetry, can make his verses easily by means of a diction which time has proved to be the best.

Expressions in the first lines of *Widsith* reflect the oral formulaic traditions of Germanic poetry. *Forman siðe* ("first," "on the first journey," "for the first time," etc.) appears frequently in Old English poetry. It occurs, for example, twice in the dative case (as in *Widsith*) in *Beowulf* (lines 740b, 2286b). In both instances, it forms a full second half-line and is not emphatic in its meaning but serves to fill out the line. One assumes it was a convenient filler when the poet was dealing with activity which could be described as "first" and he needed a second half-line alliterating on *f*. The formula can also be used in other cases, but in the nominative (*forma sið*, *Beowulf*, line 716b, etc.) it loses a syllable and, therefore, its metrical quantity changes. Thus it is absorbed into another, more emphatic formula: *ne wæs þæt forma sið* ("that was not the first time . . ."). Its reverse, *niehstan siðe*, is also used twice in the dative case in *Beowulf* (lines 1203b, 2511a) but its meaning is more emphatic than that of *forman siðe*, especially when it occurs in the first half-line as an introduction to the hero's last speech.

Forman siðe is, then, a formula, an expression which occurs, as Professor Magoun defined it, "exactly the same elsewhere or with only some insignificant change in inflection about which a singer would scarcely have to devote conscious thought in order to fit it into some different context or slightly different grammatical situation." It is also related to a formula *niehstan siðe* which is its reverse and to other formulas in which *forma* and *sið* are related but which have different metrical values. In *Beowulf*, there also occurs the expression *hindeman siðe* (lines 2049b,

2517b) which, in meaning and scansion, is equivalent to *niehstan sìðe*, except that in a second half-line it would alliterate differently. The two expressions form what is known as a formulaic system: "a group of phrases which have the same metrical value and which are enough alike in the thought and words to leave no doubt that the poet who used them knew them not only as a single formula, but also as formulas of a certain type." Formulaic systems gave the poets freedom to vary their expressions or, in the case of Old English, to fit them to their alliterative needs.

The use of *maðolade* ("made a speech") in the first line of *Widsith* is an example of another kind of formulaic diction. It is customary in Old English verse to introduce speeches, especially formal or set-speeches, with this preterite indicative verb as the second word of a first half-line. The first word is the name of the speaker serving as subject, and the second half-line—and often succeeding verses—usually describes the speaker or otherwise sets the stage for the locution which is to follow. In a given poem, formulas are frequently developed incorporating the *maðelode* expression for a speaker. So, for example, Beowulf's speeches are customarily introduced formulaically with *Beowulf maðelode, bearn Ecgþeowes* ("Beowulf spoke, the son of Ecgtheow"; lines 529, 957, 1383, 1473, 1651, 1817, 1999, 2425) and Hrothgar's with *Hroðgar maðelode, helm Scyldinga* ("Hrothgar spoke, guardian of the Scyldings"; lines 371, 456, 1321). The speech may begin after one line of formulaic introduction; or, sometimes to underline the importance of what is to be said, there may be a digression having to do with the speaker. In the introduction to Hrothgar's last speech before Beowulf's departure, for example, it is said that he examined the hilt of the sword with which Beowulf had killed Grendel's mother and the decoration of the hilt is described (lines 1687b–1699).

The use of the *maðelode* formula in *Widsith* is unusual in that, rather than describing the subject of the verb or the action, it repeats the verb with the striking *wordhord onleac*, itself probably a formulaic expression. The poet then proceeds to describe the speaker in eight lines of introductory digression which prepare the reader for the far-traveler's fabulous claims to experience and acquaintance. But, however unusual the first line of *Widsith* may be in its application of this traditional expression, it clearly looks back to the customary manner in which oral poets introduced speeches.

Maðolade is also one of a large number of words in Old English which occurs only in poetry. The fact that such words persisted in poetic diction is itself probably in part attributable to the oral-formulaic tradition of Germanic verse. Formulas tended to persist, to be used generation after generation. The remains of Continental and Icelandic poetry, which share many formulas with Old English, show that the hoard of formulas may well go back to the common pre-history of the Germanic peoples. Thus, words which passed out of usage in prose writing tended to be preserved for poetic purposes alone. Sometimes (as may be the case for beasts of battle, or rulers' names) congeries of words survived in association with traditional uses in given contexts which might themselves be called thematic—or even formulaic, in a very loose sense of the term.

Other evidence supports the belief that early Germanic poetry was oral and formulaic and hints at the method of composition and retention. The thulas of *Widsith*, for example, are probably the oldest passages which have survived in Old English. Clearly the singers who devised them were thinking in terms of pairs of half-line units. Thus the units are all end-stopped (whereas enjambment characterizes such later passages of the poem as the nine-line introduction to Widsith's speech). Syntactically, sentences follow the same pattern. Thus, in the first thula, the pattern is "*x* [nominative subject] ruled *y* [instrumental plural]." After a half-line in which the verb is used, the poet can omit it and give only the names of the ruler and of the people ruled. After line 28 (a variant of the pattern which expands it to cover a whole line by adding the adverb *lengest*), the verb is not repeated for five lines. Given this pattern, the poet was presumably able to concentrate on the groups of alliterating names he wanted to evoke without having to be overly worried about sentence structure and syntax.

In the Germanic past, as *Widsith* and other Old English poems testify, poetry had been composed orally and was characterized above all by formulism. Whether any of the extant Old English poetry was in fact so composed and then, by dictation or other means, committed to writing is another and more difficult question. Professor Francis Peabody Magoun, Jr., and his follow-

ers have argued strongly that it was. Recently, however, difficulties have been raised, and the issue seems now to be unanswered
and unanswerable. Aldhelm, bishop of Sherbourne (d. 709), is said
by William of Malmesbury to have made vernacular songs in the
traditional manner. But Aldhelm was also learned in Latin and the
producer of elaborate and florid works in what he and his contemporaries imagined to be the most sublime style. Thus at this
early date, his English style may well have been influenced by
his Latin learning, and (although none of Aldhelm's native verse
survives) there is ample evidence of Latin influence elsewhere in
Old English poetry. Latin influences would not in themselves
rule out the continuation of the oral tradition; indeed, Magoun
and his followers have tried to include the writers of Christian
poetry among the Anglo-Saxons as oral composers. But it is
probably safer to say of Old English poetry that its style is "formular," that it is profoundly aware of and influenced by the
formulaic method of the Germanic oral tradition. Whether *Beowulf*, highly formular and traditional yet also Christian, was composed orally is impossible to say. That its diction is formulaic
and that it was written deliberately in the manner of the oral
poetic tradition is certain. *Widsith,* too, looks to that tradition
and the age in which the tradition flourished; and it, at least,
combines some almost certainly ancient thulas with the artistry
of the later poet who imagined the singer Widsith and his adventures and used traditional, formular diction to describe his
character. The scribe who copied it into the Exeter anthology
at the end of the tenth century was apparently still interested
both in the content of the poem and in the fact that it was
made in the traditional way.

2. *Prosody.*

The ground on which we stand in discussing Germanic prosody is somewhat surer, but the evidence must all be gleaned from
the poetic remains themselves, since essays on prosody were not
produced by the Germanic writers. It is, however, clear that all
Germanic verse from very early times was based upon two
principles: half-lines, which had two stresses and at least one
period of unstress; and alliteration or front-rhyme, which was
used to bind half-lines into pairs or long-lines. The unstressed

periods of half-lines had a variable number of unstressed syllables which, for Old English, were required to fit one of five basic patterns of rhythm.

This is not the place to write at length about the mechanics of Anglo-Saxon and other Germanic alliterative verse, but some comments can perhaps be made about apparent general trends in the development and use of the alliterative form among the Germanic language groups.

Although one would like to know much more about the matter, the antiquity of the basic principles of alliteration can be demonstrated from an allusion in Tacitus' *Germania* and from such early runic inscriptions as that on the fourth- or fifth-century horn of Gallehus. The horn inscription is generally accepted as proof that the alliterative line dates "from before the completion of the Germanic migrations" when "few linguistic changes had taken place which would separate its language from Proto-Germanic." The alliterative line depends upon a series of stressed first syllables. There must be two stressed syllables in each half-line, and the first stressed syllable of the second half-line controls the alliteration for the whole line: that is, one or both of the stressed syllables of the first unit must alliterate with it; the second syllable of the second half-line should not alliterate. Since stress on the first syllable of words is so important to the alliterative line, it is believed that Germanic alliterative verse cannot descend from the period of the very early stage of Germanic linguistic evolution during which the accent was variable. Practice as to the length of lines varied from place to place in the Germanic linguistic areas. In the north, the half-line tends to be short, often in Old Norse containing only four syllables, two stressed and two unstressed; in the south, especially in Old Low German (Old Saxon), the lines tend to far greater diffuseness. The meaning of this fact in terms of the history of Germanic verse is, however, unclear. Recent students have argued that a median between conciseness and diffuseness was probably the original state and that, in the course of time, the northern poets tended to make their verse more terse, while those to the south, who were also working towards a greater narrative lucidity under the influence of Latin poetry, tended to relax their verse form by introducing a greater number of unstressed syllables.

This argument is hypothetical, however, for the evidence for the North-Germanic languages is quite late.

Northern and southern Germanic poetry also tended to bifurcate in terms of the genres and forms which the poets employed. The alliterative form was abandoned in favor of end-rhymed verse according to geographical considerations, southern poets adopting the Latin style of versification far earlier than those in the far north. Thus in southern German tongues, rhyme was introduced in the ninth century while alliteration persisted in Old Icelandic verse into the thirteenth century. Northern poetry tended to be stanzaic but the southern was on the whole stichic, or formed of series of alliterative long-lines.

In both northern and southern Germanic poetry, the dominant genre was what has been called *epic*, for want of a better term. The epic was usually short and more concerned with single events and their effects upon the characters involved than with narration in the usual sense. As Professor Lehmann remarks on the suitability of the term:

> Though we continue to use the term *epic*, in neither the northern nor the southern verse was there emphasis on narration until the long epic was introduced in the south on the pattern of Latin epic poetry. The Germanic audience already knew the stories. It was the task of the poet to depict the most dramatic incident in them, and its effect on the fate of the protagonists. Only in a modified sense may we, therefore, use the term *epic* to describe Germanic verse.

Prose came to be used in the north for longer narrative, and stanzaic ballads became the most important generic group of poems. Some of these ballads dealt with the heroes and gods of the Germanic past. This "Eddic poetry" is largely anonymous. Another group of poems, the "Skaldic verse," was written by known poets ("skalds") to commemorate specific events in the life and acquaintance of the singer. It was replete with allusion to Germanic mythology and assumed a wide knowledge of these matters on the part of the audience. These characteristics, combined with the terseness of the verse and its love of obscure circumlocutions, make the northern verse quite difficult for modern readers. The thulas of *Widsith* illustrate the problems. For the modern reader, they are merely lists of names, but for the poet and his audience they must have been rich in associations that are now forever lost.

Southern poetry—especially that in Old English, which belongs linguistically to the southern or West Germanic group but which, geographically, occupies a middle ground—contains enough resemblances to the Skaldic and Eddic ballad types to convince scholars that both belong to the common Germanic heritage. The preponderant remains in the southern groups are epic in proportion. With the exception of *Beowulf,* they treat biblical or hagiographic subjects in the heroic manner. In this group, one would include the Old English works of Cynewulf and his "school" and the Old Saxon *Heliand.* Thus, both subject and form testify to the strong influence of Latinity and Christianity on the Germanic tradition.

Two stylistic devices distinguish southern from northern Germanic poetry and are another kind of evidence of their historic development from the earlier norms of Germanic verse. The first is variation or repetition. Southern verse characteristically repeats itself, piling almost synonymous variant expressions atop each other. The first three and one-half lines of *Widsith* show the principle of variation at work. *Wordhord onleac* repeats *maðolade* metaphorically. *Folca* ("nations") in line 3 repeats *mægþa* ("tribes") in line 2 without changing its meaning but, perhaps, adding to the impression of the extent of Widsith's journeys. The sentence in lines 3b–4a repeats with variation lines 2a–3a by asserting not only that Widsith had traveled widely but also that he had been accepted in the highest circles. Variation strikes the student early in his experience as one of the most salient rhetorical characteristics of Old English verse.

The other stylistic device characteristic of southern verse is enjambment or the continuation of the sense and syntactic structure from one line into the next. It has already been noted that one of the marks of the early thulas of *Widsith* was that the lines were parallel in structure and end-stopped, or syntactically self-contained. But in the introduction of lines 1–9—the contribution of the author who presumably wrote in the late seventh century—enjambment predominates. Only the first sentence—and that of necessity—begins at the beginning of a line. While editors have had to add commas at the ends of lines 2, 5, and 8, the only full stops come between the first and second halves of lines 3, 4, 5, and 9. Thus *Widsith* reflects both the northern and the southern syntactical treatment of the alliterative line.

Brief allusion may be made to one last trait of Germanic poetry. The northern poets as a part of their effort to achieve conciseness and allusiveness frequently used compound words called *kennings*, which referred periphrastically or by means of circumlocution to their subject. Thus, in Old Norse, the compound which means literally "tang of the hillside" is a kenning for "grass". Such expressions are unusual in southern poetry. They also occur frequently in Old English, although the reference is not so oblique as in the strict kenning. (For this reason some scholars argue that *kend heiti* would be a more accurate term.) Examples are the famous "heath-stepper" for "stag" or "strife of waves" for "ocean" or, in *Widsith*, "word-hoard" for "vocabulary."

These geographically varying characteristics of the basic Germanic verse form demonstrate both the antiquity and traditionalism of Germanic poetry and also the fact that the poetry of the Anglo-Saxons was profoundly dependent upon the heritage of the Continental and oral period of their forebears. But they testify as well to the essential obscurity of that preliterate period. The evidence is largely ex post facto: that is, it depends upon manuscript evidence from the eighth or ninth century through the thirteenth. The poetry of the north developed in comparative isolation from Latin culture (although its written record postdates the conversion of the north), and the poetry of the south was early and profoundly influenced by Latin literature and religion. Comparison of the northern poems with the southern allows us to ascertain common characteristics of Germanic verse; but, sadly, it allows no more than conjecture about the history of the development of the verse, its content, genres, and style.

3. *Music and poetry.*

The third aspect of the background of Germanic poetry, the role of musical accompaniment, is clearly documented but only superficially understood and hypothetically reconstructed. But, again, it is an aspect which is in the background of the experience of the imaginary minstrel of *Widsith,* for, at the end of the second division or fit of the poem, Widsith speaks of the manner of poetic performance:

> When Scilling and I with clear voice raised the song before our victorious lord—loud to the harp the words sounded in harmony—then many men proud in mind, of full knowledge, said they had never heard a better song.
>
> (lines 103–108)

The passage is more difficult than illuminating. Scilling is probably the name of a second singer who may have sung antiphonally with Widsith—a practice known among Finnish singers—but it might also be the name of Widsith's harp, personified as "the Bright-toned One." One would like to know rather more exactly the meaning and musical implications of *hlude bi hearpen hleoþ or swinsade* ("loud to the harp the words sounded in harmony"), words whose precise connotations as to the manner of performance, musical dynamics, and the like are, quite simply, lost to us.

Nevertheless, the *Widsith* passage is but one piece of evidence pointing to the importance of both accompaniment and singing in Germanic oral composition and performance. Latin writers such as Sidonius (d. *c.* 479) leave the impression that the singing of Continental Germans was, to say the least, cacophonous. Bede says that Cædmon, the uncultured shepherd who became the first singer of Christian song in England, participated in feasts at the monastery of Whitby, at which the harp was passed from one participant to another. He also makes clear the fact that Cædmon, who had no training in the arts of performance and composition, could have become a gifted singer overnight only by means of a miracle. In *Beowulf,* it seems that the usual performer was the professional scop, but on occasion King Hrothgar takes the harp and sings. Two rather later poems in the Exeter Book, the *Riming Poem* (lines 24b–30) and *The Fortunes of Men* (lines 80–84), mention performances on the harp.

One Anglo-Saxon harp, excavated with the ship burial at Sutton Hoo, survives. It is a small instrument, and its reconstruction is conjectural because the fragments might fit either of two models illustrated in the manuscripts and in stone carvings: the Celtic harp or the Germanic lyre. The manners of tuning and playing the harps are also conjectural, although it is likely that they were strummed both by hand and with a plectrum.

Recently, a good deal of attention has been given to the manner in which these harps may have been used in performances. One possibility, suggested by Professor Pope, is that the harp "kept the time with a minimum of harmonic variation, sounding the main beats and perhaps contributing a few flourishes by itself at points where the narrative could be briefly suspended." The nature of the musical role of the human voice is, however, even more difficult. There may have been a basic melody, either repeated or varied; a style of delivery akin to operatic recitative is also possible; and it is also likely that melody was affected at a fairly early date by contact with Latin chant. As to the primitive musical connections of Germanic oral verse, nothing is known; but it seems fair to guess that the earlier tendency to use end-stopped lines and the strict two-stress structure of the alliterative half-line were conducive to recitation with the assistance of the harp.

The formulaic nature of Old English poetic rhetoric, its versification, and its frequent reference to musical accompaniment, then, are all facets of the Germanic poetic tradition kept alive, although greatly modified, in the literary period under consideration in this book. Far less than we should like is known about the oral period of Germanic development, but it is clear that both the debt and the continuity are considerable. Elements—some of them extremely important—of classical influence on this Germanic verse will be considered later; but for the moment it should only be added that the changes are quite as important to a full appreciation of the literature as the continuities.

C. The Germanic Social and Cultural Heritage

Thus far, this inquiry into the nature of the importance of the Germanic heritage in the life and literature of England before the Conquest of 1066 has established—however inferentially and circumstantially—that the Anglo-Saxons never lost a sense of their ethnic identity as descendants of the Germanic peoples of the

Heroic Age and that the form of their poetry remained markedly Germanic. The obvious next question is whether and to what extent Germanic social forms and institutions continued among this people whose nostalgia for their past so colored their culture long after their conversion to Christianity.

In this connection one turns almost instinctively to *Beowulf*, that great evocation of the Germanic, heroic past by a Christian singer or imitator of the ancient poetic style. It is a poem of the earlier part of the Anglo-Saxon period but one which was copied and read in the period under discussion. In *Beowulf*, we have what purports to be a re-creation of the heroic age with historically verifiable touchstones such as the references to Hrothgar's Heorot, celebrated in lines 45–49 of *Widsith*, and the death of Higelac, which is also reported by the most authoritative Latin historian of the age, Gregory of Tours, in his *History of the Franks*. Thus it is inevitable that scenes of social life in the great Old English epic should have been ransacked for their reminiscences of Germanic social life and cultural presuppositions. Among the many passages which invite this kind of attention, none have been more popular than the great banquet scenes of the first half of the poem, replete with the lavish exchange of gifts, professions of honor and loyalty between kings and their retainers and visitors, and striking examples both of the love for song and of the content of the verse recited on such occasions.

Of these scenes, the one which intervenes between Beowulf's defeat of Grendel and his encounter with the monster's mother is both the most complete and the most celebrated:

> Then it was time
> for Healfdene's son to proceed to the hall,
> the king himself was eager to attend the feast.
> I have never heard of a greater band of kinsmen
> gathered with such dignity around their ring-giver.
> Then the glorious warriors sat on the benches,
> rejoicing in the feast. Courteously
> their kinsmen, Hrothgar and Hrothulf,
> quaffed many a mead-cup, confident warriors
> in the high hall. Heorot was packed
> with feasters who were friends; the time was not yet come
> when the Scyldings practised wrongful deeds.

Then Hrothgar gave Beowulf Healfdene's sword,
and a battle banner, woven with gold,
and a helmet and a corslet, as rewards for victory;
many men watched while the priceless, renowned sword
was presented to the hero. Beowulf emptied
the ale-cup in the hall; he had no cause
to be ashamed at those precious gifts.
There are few men, as far as I have heard,
who have given four such treasures, gleaming with gold,
to another on the mead-bench with equal generosity.
A jutting ridge, wound about with metal wires,
ran over the helmet's crown, protecting the skull,
so that well-ground swords, proven in battle,
could not injure the well-shielded warrior
when he advanced against his foes.
Then the guardian of thanes ordered
that eight horses with gold-plated bridles
be led into the courtyard; onto one was strapped
a saddle, inlaid with jewels, skillfully made.
That was the war-seat of the great king,
Healfdene's son, whenever he wanted
to join in the sword-play. That famous man
never lacked bravery at the front in battle,
when men about him were cut down like corn.
Then the king of the Danes, Ing's descendants,
presented the horses and weapons to Beowulf,
bade him use them well and enjoy them.
Thus the renowned prince, the retainers' gold-warden,
rewarded those fierce sallies in full measure,
with horses and treasure, so that no man
would ever find reason to reproach him fairly.
Furthermore, the guardian of warriors gave
a treasure, an heirloom at the mead-bench,
to each of those men who had crossed the sea
with Beowulf; and he ordered that gold
be paid for that warrior Grendel slew
so wickedly—as he would have slain many another,
had not foreseeing God and the warrior's courage
together forestalled him. The Creator ruled over
all humankind, even as He does today.
Wherefore a wise man will value forethought
and understanding. Whoever lives long

on earth, endures the unrest of these times,
will be involved in much good and much evil.
    Then Hrothgar, leader in battle, was entertained
with music—harp and voice in harmony.
The strings were plucked, many a song rehearsed,
when it was the turn of Hrothgar's poet
to please men at the mead-bench, perform in the hall.
He sang of Finn's troop, victims of surprise attack,
and of how that Danish hero, Hnæf of the Scyldings,
was destined to die among the Frisian slain.

                    (lines 1008b–1070)

    A people is as one in the flush of victory, and, despite the depredations of Grendel, they have the wherewithal both to reward Beowulf handsomely for his boon and to treat the visitor and his band in the highest tradition of courtly hospitality. The entertainment is as rich as the setting and the gifts; and, one knows from what has gone before and will follow, the whole occasion is marked by punctiliously decorous formal speeches and other niceties of etiquette. But the poet interrupts his description to reflect forebodingly on the time to come when the Scyldings will not be so worthy. Midway through the scene, he reflects on the deliverance from fate which the Danes had experienced through the agency of Beowulf and goes on to moralize in a distinctly Christian manner on the workings of divine providence.

    One is, in other words, dealing with a text which purports to report or depict the Germanic, pagan past but which is patently Christian in its point of view. The richness of the setting strikes the reader as either antique or romantic or both. Thus, one is met with an apparent contradiction between what was for the eighth-century poet antique-pagan and modern-Christian. If this does not in itself undermine one's confidence in the historical verity of the scene, the work of modern historical critics and archaeologists should. The latter, chiefly on the evidence of the Sutton Hoo ship burial, have shown that the cultural affluence depicted in *Beowulf* might well duplicate the conditions in the Anglo-Saxon kingdoms in which *Beowulf* was written. And the former have shown that many other social, legal, and cultural details tend as much to reflect the world as known to the audience of the *Beowulf* poet as to reconstruct the world of Germanic paganism in the first half of the sixth century.

One must reckon with the fact that the poet who recorded *Beowulf* was not a scientific historian who tried accurately to re-create the past but a medieval moralizer and teller of tales who adapted a tale from the past to his present experience. Later poets (the author of the *Nibelungenlied*, for example) presented Germanic legendary materials in chivalric dress. By depicting legendary figures in a setting which resembled their own world, they made an implicit judgment on their own times and manners. One would hesitate to say that Chaucer, by intruding "modern" dress and sentiment in *Troilus and Criseyde* or the *Knight's Tale*, had exactly the same intention, actually made a picture of fourteenth-century life, or achieved the same effects as the *Beowulf* and *Nibelungenlied* poets. Nevertheless he does not portray pagan antiquity. The *Beowulf* poet was curiously aware that he was treating a pagan people from his own Christian point of view, but it is quite clear that, if he portrays something of early Germanic life as it actually had been, the result may as easily be accidental as intentional.

There is very little evidence by which we can judge whether or not this is the case. There are, to be sure, two famous classical writings which describe the Germans who confronted Rome on its northern frontiers in the first centuries B.C. and A.D.: Julius Caesar in his report to his Roman constituents on his Gallic wars of 58–51 B.C. and Cornelius Tacitus in a treatise of A.D. 98 entitled *Germania*.

Students of Germanic culture and of Old English literature alike have been deeply indebted to these ancient works, and especially to the latter. From the *Germania*, one gets, above all, a picture of a society based on and cemented by bonds of loyalty which arise from familial or pseudo-familial (tribal) ties. It is a society which is, on the whole, warlike, honorable, democratic, moderate but vigorous and morally admirable. It is also, for Tacitus, culturally primitive. Thus it has looked very like the society of the heroic age of the Germanic peoples as depicted by the Old English poets and has been regarded by students of the poetry as evidence of what Germanic life must have been like before its "contamination" by the Christian religion. Even recent writers such as Professor Greenfield, more sympathetic to the Christianity of the Anglo-Saxons, have spoken, in discussing Christian references to the ideal of loyalty, of "the fusion of the ancient Germanic ideal described by Tacitus with the Christian idealism of eighth-century England."

This approach discounts the severe difficulties which must be met before these classical writings can be applied to Germanic society in the fifth and following centuries. In the first place, both Caesar and Tacitus are remote in time and place, writing during the earlier stages of the migrations and about Germanic tribes which generally lived farther to the south than those from whom the Anglo-Saxons were descended. Furthermore, both (and particularly Tacitus, who is most important as the chronicler of the depravity of Roman society at the end of the first century of the Empire) had strong biases against the kinds of moral turpitude and physical softness which seemed to them, as to many in our own times, inherent in urban culture. Both were probably influenced by the Latin Stoics' fulminations against the effects of sophistication on human nature and hence idealized the semi-nomadic, warlike, simple peoples on the frontiers of the Empire. Caesar even remarks quite candidly that the closer the barbarians approached the centers of Roman culture the less admirable and virile they became. One might add that something akin to this very tradition of "ethnographical romanticism" was communicated to the Christian Anglo-Saxons by writers like Jerome, Augustine, and Orosius, who made the Stoic distrust of culture a part of the orthodox Christian explanation of the vicissitudes to which civilizations such as Rome's are prone. They linked that view with the Old Testament prophets' charge that God imposes retributive justice upon those who stray from the straight and narrow path of the covenant. By the time *Beowulf* was composed and again during a kind of revival of the heroic in the tenth century, the Anglo-Saxon intellectuals shared with Caesar and Tacitus a romanticized vision of primitive Germanic society. Neither the Romans nor the Anglo-Saxons were cultural anthropologists.

The ancient sources are hardly reliable guides to the nature of Germanic life before and at the time of the migration of the Anglo-Saxons to Britain, and the points at which they intersect with later evidence can as well be attributed to coincidence as to historicity. Having issued this strong warning, however, one can also acknowledge that Caesar and Tacitus, with a few less well-known Latin writers, are almost the only evidence we have and that they still command our attention.

Two features in particular struck nineteenth-century students as they read the *Germania* and other documents related to early Teutonic history: the assertions that members of Germanic society enjoyed considerable personal freedom and that the king, elected by a council, was subject to the limitations of customary law. Romantically, these historians tried to see in early Germanic history a proto-democracy, the development of which was arrested by feudalism, monarchism, and (often) Christianity. A series of events, ranging from the Magna Carta, the Reformation, the revolution against the Stuarts, and the restraints placed on the crown by the Restoration and Glorious Revolution to the rise of enlightened liberalism seemed to most of these historians to be reassertions of the basic virtues of Germanic society which had been undermined by Roman law and the Roman church. In what Professor Herbert Butterfield calls "the Whig interpretation of history," the origin of the liberal doctrine of democratic freedom was, in other words, "expounded in the light of primitive Germanic freedom."

Another difficulty to which more recent historians and historical critics have directed our attention is that the descendants of the Germanic peoples tended, as did disgruntled Romans like Caesar and Tacitus, to romanticize their ancestors. Documents like *Beowulf* look back to a golden age during which men of heroic stature and indomitably right wills battled against insuperable and irrational forces. From the little we know of Germanic history in the period before the Anglo-Saxon settlement, the struggles of that age were great, but it is questionable whether the purposiveness and puissance of the figures involved were quite so impressive as a later age imagined. Any reader, say, of Gregory of Tours' *History of the Franks* must surely wonder whether, despite the author's prejudices, the prototype of the Hygelac of *Beowulf* can have been any more heroic than the feckless Merovingians who overpowered him.

The age of the great legendary and mythological figures is known as the heroic age. The similarities of the Germanic heroic age to the heroic era depicted in the Homeric epics have often been noted, and one might also point to the so-called J and S documents of the Pentateuch as an analogous depiction of the heroic age of an ethnic group. The heroic age can be defined as a formative period—the period of the settlement and emergence of a people as an identifiable and self-conscious ethnic unit; viewed from a period of more complex civilization, it seemed to have embodied the ideals and standards of conduct which were still taken as axiomatic but not often realized. Thus both the historic personages and the fictitious and mythological figures who populate the heroic age as it is recalled in later literature are larger than life and (usually despite superhuman odds and often with tragic results) epitomize both a simpler and purer level of cultural development and an ideal of conduct. The characters in *Beowulf* who attend the banquet after the defeat of Grendel appear in a setting which is in many ways recognizable to most members of the audience; but the magnificence of the setting and occasion and the nobility of the characters are so idealized as to be beyond the emulation of the hearers of the tale at the same time as they represent the standards for which those hearers feel they should strive.

Students of mythology used to believe that the mythic and legendary tales of the heroic age which came to be enshrined in the epic poetry of a later age were developed from a core of historic truth. According to this view, if the hero of *Beowulf* is fictitious, he is also the representative personification of his people at a certain stage of their history. Thus, if one knows how to distinguish the mythic from the historical, the heroic literature has considerable value as historic documentation. More recent mythographers, under the influence of Carl Jung, have tended to see the sources of myth as religious or, more specifically, cultic. Thus, A. Margaret Arent has written:

> In contrast to former romantic explanations which superficially equated the fantasy motifs with mythical conceptions and the heroes with nature deities to account for the symbolic content of the *Heldensage*, the newer "mythological" interpretations reach back to beliefs lived and enacted in cult practices, to universal thought patterns in the human psyche ["archetypes"] that derive from a sacred rather than a profane experiencing of the world. . . .
>
> The essential themes associated with the heroic tradition can be traced back to the typical course of a warrior's life formed by

cult practices. These forms crystallized into *topoi* and developed independently in the plastic and literary arts (traditional oral patterns no doubt preceding those which appear already firmly established in the early written literature).

Since the archetypal patterns for the hero's life are the same, at least within the Indo-European areas and probably even more widely, they testify not so much to the history of a specific ethnic group as to the psychic experience of man as objectified in his cultus. And if the heroic literature has any value for the historian, it will lie in his analysis of the appropriation of the myth by the author of the version under examination. Thus, for example, the mythographer would look to *Beowulf* not so much for evidence of Germanic history and religion as for the manner in which the mythic materials are appropriated by the poet. Following this line of reasoning, Professor Arent concluded that the Christian *Beowulf* poet has infused the archetypal hero pattern with new vitality because of his concern to elucidate the heroic life in the light of his own religious convictions. For other medieval authors who turned to Germanic mythic materials with no such motives, the archetypal pattern sometimes became a mere stereotype or conventional form of action and plot development.

Archaeology provides a surer source of information, but its findings to date, largely evidence based on graves and grave goods, are not very helpful in drawing the kind of social and religious picture of pre-Christian Saxon society the student of poetry would like to have. They testify, as do written records, to the use of both inhumation and cremation. Grave goods are abundant and invite speculation as to Germanic belief in an afterlife, but the evidence is not univocal, and furthermore archaeologists do not always agree in their interpretations of the evidence. The objects recovered by archaeology do, however, hint at a sophisticated and affluent culture, closely akin to what one hears described in *Beowulf*. Early medieval archaeology—a comparatively young field in which much work is now being done and reported—is the one field which promises to bring forth more information about the nature of Germanic society, custom, and culture.

The banqueting scene at Heorot, like much of the rest of *Beowulf*, then, evokes the splendor in physical wealth and in magnanimity of spirit of a lost and heroic age and stresses communal harmony. It belongs, in the archetypal pattern, to the motif of the rewards which accrue to the hero. But primarily it is more the creation of a fertile imagination working on traditional themes than a product either of disciplined historical investigation or of the folk-memory. For the Christian poet it depicts a time of achievement and pride in a life which is characterized both by such moments and by moments of defeat and despair:

> Whoever lives long
> on earth, endures the unrest of these times,
> will be involved in much good and much evil.

This chapter has been in many ways a negative report, the thesis of which is that only a very few facts—and those extremely difficult to evaluate—are known about the Germanic heritage of the Anglo-Saxons, although to the Anglo-Saxons themselves throughout their history that heritage seemed in sentiment and in fact a very important aspect of their being. If I have perhaps overstated the case, it is because I believe that it is necessary for students of Old English to be far more cautious in this regard than they have been in the past. The only picture of the Germanic background of Anglo-Saxon society which can be constructed with any certainty is of that which existed in the aftermath of the conversion to Christianity. Anything else is largely hypothetical.

Something about the reasons for our lack of knowledge about pre-Christian Anglo-Saxon history other than the mere paucity of the evidence may be offered by way of conclusion. Professor Hugh Trevor-Roper once opened a series of lectures on medieval history with the following, deliberately polemical remarks:

> It is fashionable to speak today as if European history were devalued: as if historians, in the past, have paid too much attention to it; and as if, nowadays, we should pay less. Undergraduates, seduced, as always, by the changing breath of journalistic fashion, demand that they should be taught the history of black Africa. Perhaps, in the future, there will be some African history to teach. But at present there is none, or very little: there is only

the history of the Europeans in Africa. The rest is largely darkness, like the history of pre-European, pre-Columbian America. And darkness is not a subject for history.

Given the current appeal of African, black, and other "area studies," these words sound repulsively smug and even chauvinistic. But it is true that Western (Christian) culture is uniquely marked by the notion that history is dynamic and purposeful, that social institutions are subject to change for better or worse. Without arguing whether, say, Chinese or African culture had any such concepts before they were confronted with the culture of the West, we must admit, at least, that non-Western cultures have been radically changed as a result of that meeting. Without it, Chinese communism and Indian democracy and the effort of the African states to develop so that they can deal as equals with the "developed" nations would be inconceivable. If these and other factors are the necessary concomitants of history, Trevor-Roper is quite right in saying that history was something the non-Western world did not have before it met the West.

The same can be said of the Germanic peoples. They moved from a culture which left only the merest traces and were swallowed up by the institutions which provided continuity with classical civilization during the Early Middle Ages. Traits survived —perhaps still survive—which differentiated the Anglo-Saxon from other Europeans, but those traits were for the most part superficial and accidental. It was nevertheless important for the Anglo-Saxon to try to understand himself in the setting of Europe and Christianity in terms of his Germanic origins—rather as it has become important for the black in America to understand himself as an Afro-American. But the Afro-American cannot recapture, re-create, or even accurately reconstruct his African past, let alone his exact tribal origins. The ethnic self-consciousness of the Anglo-Saxon was something like that, although it did not involve the same degree of suffering as the Afro-American's experience: it was an attempt to hold onto one half of his background in order to understand where he stood within a Western and Christian civilization which was also the inheritor of Greco-Roman culture.

To assert, as did the late R. W. Chambers, that, had the unrecorded songs of the oral singers been captured in manuscript, "the homilies and lives of saints which bulk so largely in Medieval

English verse and prose, would subside till they occupied a just, and a small, proportion of our attention," is probably to miss the point. However much oral song has undoubtedly been lost, the fact is not that the Anglo-Saxons in the literary period of their history were Germans with a thin veneer of Christianity but that they were Christians of fairly remote German ethnic origin. It is almost miraculous that we have verse in Old English—let alone that a significant portion of it reflects Germanic lore and poetic form. We are lucky to have what we have, and we probably have it precisely because the mixture of materials from the homilies to *Widsith* accurately reflects the total cultural life of the Anglo-Saxons. It is impossible to know how much more the tenth-century Anglo-Saxons to whom we owe the preservation of most of the verse, both "Germanic" and Christian, knew of Germanic lore and history than we do. But it is conceivable that, comparatively, we stand in the better position for understanding their ethnic background and assimilation into European culture.

III. Early Medieval Christianity

T HE PRECEDING CHAPTER CONSIDERED ASPECTS OF THE
Germanic background of Old English literature. The present is a
consideration of aspects of Latin-classical-Christian culture as it
was preserved in the Early Middle Ages. It has already been
stated that the treatment of these facets of the background of
Old English literature in isolation is artificial, but it is a necessary
prolegomenon to consideration of the fused culture of the Anglo-
Saxon Christian.

A. MONASTICISM AND CHRISTIAN CULTURE

The religious history of England in the tenth and eleventh
centuries radiates from the activities of King Edgar (959-975) and
three ecclesiastical advisers: Dunstan (d. 988), Abbot of Glaston-
bury, then successively Bishop of Worcester and London and
Archbishop of Canterbury; Æthelwold (d. 984), Abbot of Abing-
don before he became Bishop of Winchester; and Oswald (d. 992),
Bishop of Worcester and Archbishop of York. The following passage is from the introduction to the *Regularis Concordia,* issued
around 970 by Edgar to codify the program of monastic reform
which he had been actively supporting:

> 1. Edgar the glorious, by the grace of Christ illustrious King
> of the English and of the other peoples dwelling within the bounds
> of the island of Britain, from his earliest years began to fear, love
> and worship God with all his heart. . . . Wherefore, lest the spark

of faith, which was beginning gradually to brighten, should be extinguished by sloth and idleness, he began carefully and earnestly to consider by what holy and deserving works it could be made to burn with the brilliance and ardour of perfection.

2. When therefore he learned that the holy monasteries in all quarters of his kingdom, brought low, and almost wholly lacking in the service of our Lord Jesus Christ, were wasting away and neglected, moved by the grace of the Lord he most gladly set himself to restore them everywhere to their former good estate. Wherefore he drove out the negligent clerks with their abominations, placing in their stead for the service of God, throughout the length and breadth of his dominions, not only monks but also nuns, under abbots and abbesses; and these, out of gratitude to God, he enriched with all good things.

3. Thus, in the fulfillment of his royal office, even as the Good Shepherd, he carefully rescued and defended from the savage open mouths of the wicked—as it were the gaping jaws of wolves—those sheep which by God's grace he had diligently gathered together. . . .

4. When therefore the Rule of the holy Father Benedict had been accepted with the greatest goodwill, very many of the abbots and abbesses with their communities of monks and nuns vied with one another in following in the footsteps of the saints. . . . Exceedingly delighted with such great zeal the aforesaid king, after deep and careful study of the matter, commanded a Synodal Council to be held at Winchester. . . .

5. Straightway, then, [those who had been summoned by "a letter, set forth magnificently on parchment and couched in encouraging and peaceable terms"] obeyed his commands with the utmost gladness; and calling to mind the letters in which our holy patron Gregory instructed the blessed Augustine that, for the advancement of the rude English Church, he should establish therein the seemly customs of the Gallic Churches as well as those of Rome, they summoned monks from St Benedict's monastery at Fleury and from that eminent monastery which is known by the renowned name of Ghent, gathered from their praiseworthy customs much that was good and thus, even as honey is gathered by bees from all manner of wild flowers and collected into one hive, so also the said monastic customs, tempered by great and subtle judgment of reason were, by the grace of Christ the Saviour of the world, embodied in this small book. . . .

This remarkable passage alludes to three aspects of the late Anglo-Saxon monastic tradition which must be understood in some detail by all students of the literature of the period: the role of Gregory the Great in the conversion of Saxon England, the position of Benedict of Nursia as the father of Western monasticism, and the international phenomenon of monastic reform in the tenth century.

The importance of Gregory is best understood in the perspective provided by Bede, for it is through Bede's account that later Englishmen derived their knowledge of his work. The first of the five books of Bede's *Ecclesiastical History* is devoted to the history of Christianity in Britain to 603, only a few years after the arrival of Roman missionaries in 597. Bede opens with a description of Britain and Ireland, an account of the settlement, and a report of the vicissitudes and successes of Christianity in Roman Britain. He recounts the difficulties encountered by the Britons and Romans in the face of harassment by tribes to the north. The Roman legions having by this time been withdrawn to the Continental frontiers, Bede says that in 449 the British leader Vortigern granted land in return for military assistance to "the Angles or Saxons" who, in fact, were more interested in attacking than protecting the Britons (I. 5). After driving the Scots invaders back to the north, the Anglo-Saxons invited their fellows on the Continent to join them, "adding that the country was fertile and the Britons cowardly." Bede goes on to describe the newcomers as being "from the three most formidable races of Germany, the Saxons, Angles, and Jutes" and adds something concerning the manner in which they settled themselves across Britain. Like the Chronicler much later, he mentions Hengest and Horsa as the first leaders and as descendants of Woden (whom Bede does not recognize as a deity). It was not long before the Anglo-Saxons turned on the Britons, many of whom were Christians; Bede regards the Britons' suffering as divine retribution for their sins and the pagans (like the Chaldeans who warred against Jerusalem) as instruments of God's wrath. For more than a century, the fate of the Britons was miserable and relieved only by the examples of a small number of loyal and courageous bishops.

The problem as Bede poses it, then, is not of the conversion of Britain so much as the restoration of Christianity to the island. Thus, he sees the stage set for a new period of Christian missionary activity: "But God in his goodness did not utterly abandon the people whom he had chosen, for he remembered them, and sent this nation more worthy preachers of truth to bring them to the Faith" (I. 22). These "more worthy preachers" were, of course, the mission of monks from Rome sent by Pope Gregory the Great to the kingdom of Kent in 597. As the drama continues to unfold, the restoration of Christianity to Britain tends to take the form of the conversion of the Germanic settlers and of competition (particularly in the north) between the Celtic Christianity of the British and Irish and the Roman customs of the missionaries. Ultimately Roman forms won the day; and so it is fitting that Bede concludes his history (V. 22) with the submission in 716 of the last important dissidents, the monks of the Isle of Iona.

Although Celtic influences continued to be felt throughout the Anglo-Saxon period, the Roman victory can, for present purposes, be regarded as virtually complete. Gregory the Great became the most important patron of English churchmen. To the anonymous monk of Whitby who wrote the first *Life of Gregory* a decade or two before Bede, he was the Apostle of the English:

> When all the Apostles bring their own peoples with them and each individual teacher brings his own race to present them to the Lord in the Day of Judgment, he will bring us—that is, the English people—instructed by him through God's grace; and we believe this to be all the more wonderful because, though absent in the body yet present in the spirit, through his divinely given apostolic powers he bravely entered the house of the strong man whom Christ had bound taking as spoil those goods, that is, ourselves, who were "sometimes darkness but now are light in the Lord."

Gregory was, in a word, "the apostle and teacher of our race."

Born in Rome about 540 to a distinguished Christian family of senatorial rank, Gregory lived during a troubled period in the history of that city. Rome was conquered by the Goth Totila in 546 and 549, restored to the power of the Byzantine emperor Justinian each time, and harried by the Germanic Lombards throughout the last three decades of the century. Gregory spent the early years of his manhood in civil service, serving at one time as urban Prefect—the chief administrative officer in Rome. He disposed of his inheritance by establishing monasteries on his Sicilian estates, making a monastery of the family townhouse on the Caelian Hill, and giving the surplus to the poor. For a time in the 570s, Gregory was apparently a monk in the community he had founded in his family home, but he reentered what he liked to call the turbulence of life in the world when he was made a Deacon of the Roman church by Benedict I. Later, he served Pope Pelagius II as *apocrisarius* or ambassador to Constantinople. He was back in Rome, perhaps as abbot on the Caelian Hill when Pelagius died in the midst of a plague and a renewed Lombard threat in 590. Elected Pope by the Roman populace, Gregory at first refused the election and tried to hide —as bishops-elect often did in token of their humility. He began his pontificate with a great public ceremony of penance, a contemporary account of which is preserved by Gregory of Tours.

It is difficult to know whether the apparent vigor of Gregory's pontificate was as truly remarkable for the time as it seems or whether this impression is in part the result of its remarkably full documentation. Probably Gregory could have held his own in any age. He seems to be the last great example of the sensitively intelligent, morally motivated, and efficiently activist Roman. Although his reforms apparently did not long survive him, they were an important model in later ages. Among his achievements were sound administration of the Roman See, forceful assertion of its primacy, usurpation of civil functions in order to preclude the vacuum threatened by the impotency of the Emperors at Constantinople, and an amazingly broad and well-informed correspondence with lay and ecclesiastical leaders from Jerusalem to Seville and Canterbury to Carthage which covers topics from the management of farms to the expectation that Doomsday is at hand. All of this was the work of a man who described himself as sickly and constantly yearned to retreat to monastic seclusion.

In addition, Gregory left a corpus of writings which exerted an enormous influence throughout the Early Middle Ages. Most important, though now least readable, is the great exegetical commentary or *Moralia* on the book of Job. There are other works of biblical exegesis, a course of sermons on Ezekiel, and forty great sermons on the Gospels of the Mass which were often read and anthologized in homiliaries or collections of sermons for the Christian year. Two shorter works were held in very high regard. The *Regula Pastoralis* or *Rule for Pastors* (i.e., bishops) is a handbook or rule of life for spiritual leaders. At times in the Early Middle Ages it was given to bishops at their consecrations along with the canon law, and a copy of the Old English translation was supplied by King Alfred to all his bishops. The *Dialogues*, concerned with miracles performed in Italy by numerous ascetics, was very popular and is also to be found among the works translated from Latin to Old English in the reign of Alfred the Great. Gregory is also associated traditionally with liturgical reform, and one of the books frequently ascribed to him is the *Liber Antiphonariis*. His authorship of this work is dubious (if only because his other works display so little interest in liturgy and music), although it was believed by the liturgical scholars in the ninth and tenth centuries that Gregorian chant was developed by Gregory I.

If his furtherance of monasticism was perhaps not Gregory's greatest work, his use of monks as missionaries to the Anglo-Saxons was his single most influential act in determining the future of Christian culture and institutions. Early medieval Christianity, especially in England, was monastic Christianity; and a good deal of knowledge about monasticism is basic to the study of English culture and literature before 1066.

Monasticism, the roots of which are traced to the life and activity of Antony of Egypt (*c.* 251–356), received the first impetus for its growth from the widespread reaction to the success of Christianity in the Roman Empire. In the period of persecution, which ran from the beginnings into the fourth century, those who were rigorous in their practice of the new religion were often given the opportunity to suffer for their faith the ultimate sacrifice of martyrdom (the word means "witness"). The martyrs were universally regarded by other Christians as a separate, heroic class. "The blood of the martyrs is the seed of the church," Tertullian had declared.

The recognition of Christianity as a permissible religion in the Empire and its eventual adoption as the official religion had two effects. First, it was no longer possible to make that special witness to the faith which persecution had afforded; and those who were most serious about their profession of Christianity were nostalgic for the lost, heroic witness. Second, in the process of absorbing a large number of nominal Christians who found it either necessary or expedient to follow the religious lead of the Emperors, the Church became secularized, or transformed from a revolutionary sect to an established institution. This process also contributed to the discontent of the rigorists.

The monastic movement was, at least in its origins, probably a response to this situation. In place of the heroic martyrdom of the age of persecution, it offered the metaphorical martyrdom of an abandonment of the world by means of a rigorously disciplined (ascetic) life. The first exemplars of the movement are known as the Desert Fathers because of the fact that they abandoned urban society for the loneliness and difficulty of life in the waste places. (They never, of course, forgot the fact that Christ had fasted and suffered temptation in the desert.) These anchorites—as the solitary ascetics were called—did not long maintain their solitude, however; for they seem so to have epitomized widely shared religious aspirations that many—often the most extremely ascetical—attracted disciples and were forced to improvise a discipline or rule of life for a community of ascetics. Hence cenobitic—or community-oriented—monasticism arose and tended, particularly in the West, to become the norm.

At first (and indeed, for a long time) monastic communities attracted members by the fame, ascetic example, and reputation for miracles of their founders. Each monastery was an independent community with its own rule, although the rules of especially famous leaders tended to influence other establishments. Rather later, in reaction against the tendencies of monasticism to ascetic and doctrinal excesses, a number of church leaders outlined moderate rules which became normative, but local variations in practice rather than uniformity characterized monastic uses throughout the Early Middle Ages.

Perhaps the most important change wrought by the regularization of monasticism was, however, undetected at the time. Monasticism had originally been an abandonment of cultivated, urbane life for a disciplined but wild and unsure life of poverty in exile from society. It was usually both anti-intellectual and anti-ecclesiastical. As it attracted more attention, however, and as cenobitic as opposed to anchoritic monasticism became the norm, it tended to become less obdurate in its opposition to the prevailing standards of the church and the society. Then, as— from the age of Augustine onwards—life in the Empire became less and less secure, the monastery began to appear to men as the one ordered place in which a devout, relatively stable, and even cultured Christian life could be pursued. It was Gregory the Great who made this point most clearly when, torn from monastic life to the prelacy, he complained that

> as I compare what I have lost with what I must now endure, the contrast only makes my present lot more burdensome. I am tossed about on the waves of a heavy sea, and my soul is like a helpless ship buffeted by raging winds. When I recall my former way of life, it is as though I were once more looking back toward land and sighing as I beheld the shore. It only saddens me the more to find that, while flung about by the mighty waves that carry me along, I can hardly catch sight any longer of the harbor I have left. (*Dialogues*, I. Preface)

The monastery became not so much a symbol of the negation of the values of culture as the one place left in the world in which a devout and cultured Christian life could be pursued.

Gregory himself advanced the situation another important step when he employed monks as his missionaries to the Anglo-Saxons, thereby entrusting them with the work of the "secular" church. The English and Irish followed suit with their own missions to the Continent. This situation tended to eclipse secular Christianity and to help make monastic or "regular" Christianity dominant throughout the Early Middle Ages. It also laid the groundwork for the celebrated situation in which monasticism became the chief preserver and purveyor of learning and literary culture.

The practices of monasticism as an institution are, unfortunately, difficult to define for the period before 800, when an important series of reforms was begun by Benedict of Aniane under the sponsorship of the Carolingian emperor Louis the Pious. Recent study—the conclusions of which are still being absorbed by scholars—has shown that the old textbook picture of monasticism from the death of St. Benedict in the middle of the sixth century to the beginning of the ninth century was vastly over-simplified. That older version, as Professor Knowles paraphrases it, saw Benedict himself as "a lawgiver of genius, who, while taking many hints from the Fathers and early monastic legis-lators, had produced an eminently original code that reflected the author's originality at every point." It was generally thought either that the *Rule of St. Benedict* was widely influential in the author's lifetime or that it came to the attention of a wide audience after Benedict's monastery at Monte Cassino had been destroyed by the Lombards (*c.* 585), forcing a number of the inmates to flee to Rome with the original copy of the *Rule*. It was assumed that Gregory the Great's own monastery was Bene-dictine, that the Pope devoted the whole of the second of four books of the *Dialogues* to Benedict because of the great monastic legislator's unique and universally recognized preeminence, that the monasticism exported by Gregory to the Anglo-Saxons was none other than that of Benedict, and that, soon thereafter, Benedict's *Rule* became the norm in the monasteries of the West.

It is now clear, however, that Benedict's *Rule* is not so origi-nal as used to be thought but that it is an adaptation of an earlier, and (in some respects) far less sophisticated monastic rule, the *Rule of the Master,* an Italian work of the early sixth century. Furthermore, it is now widely accepted that the emphasis put by Gregory on Benedict in the *Dialogues* is fortuitous and that it was not, as often used to be urged, part of an effort to propagandize the *Rule.* Indeed, although Gregory knew of the *Rule's* existence, it may be doubted whether he knew its con-tents intimately, and denied that the *Rule* was in force at Greg-ory's monastery or elsewhere in Rome.

Each monastic house in this period was an independent in-stitution. Although there were groups of houses with similarities of practice and powerful monasteries which exercised an im-portant influence, there was no uniformity of practice. There was sufficient "family" resemblance among most western European monasteries, however, to make it superficially credible that a single rule prevailed. When Bede describes the regulations which were followed at his own monastery, Monkwearmouth-Jarrow, under Benedict Biscop (died *c.* 690), it is quite clear that the customs there were eclectic. On his deathbed, Biscop is said to have claimed to have compiled his rule from no fewer than seventeen earlier *regulae* observed by foundations he had visited during his many and extensive peregrinations. This sort of eclecticism was standard practice in western monasticism before the ninth century.

Nevertheless, the Benedictine Rule was made famous by Gregory's *Dialogues;* the name of Benedict became a favorite among monks; and probably a number of monks began to believe that their rule of life was that of the Abbot of Monte Cassino. One of the great disseminators of this idea was the Anglo-Saxon Willibald who in 729 stopped on his return from a pilgrimage in the East at the newly reestablished monastery at Monte Cassino and stayed there for a decade, assisting materially in the establishment of the customs of the house. His monastic-missionary work with Boniface later in his career surely helped to spread the mystique of Benedict, Benedictinism, and Monte Cassino. Charlemagne and his ecclesiastical advisers, who had a distinct predilection for making customs uniform throughout the realm, discovered that there was no single monastic way of life but a very confusing multiplicity. They therefore sent to Monte Cassino for a copy of the *Rule* of Benedict. It is from this copy made at Charlemagne's request that the main line of the textual tradition descends. The work of the Carolingians and of a number of monastic reformers in the tenth century finally made Benedictinism (strictly so-called) the monastic norm. Ironically, it was quite late in this process—the tenth century—that the Benedictine *Rule* began to influence monasteries in Rome and to be adopted by them.

As for Anglo-Saxon monasticism, several hasty generalizations may be ventured. First, the tensions between Celtic and Roman monastic practices were settled by the triumph of the Roman at the synod of Whitby in 664. Thereafter, monasticism of a generally Roman type prevailed; it was reinforced and enriched by a constant stream of monastic travelers to and from Rome and other centers on the Continent. Second, it is likely that, in the seventh century and later, the interest in Gregory the Great in England generated interest in Benedict which, in turn, was communicated to the Continent by the Anglo-Saxon missionaries and thereby influenced the development of Carolingian monastic policy. Third, the history of Anglo-Saxon monasticism was disastrously disrupted by the Viking raiders, who seem to have made a specialty of robbing, sacking, and burning monasteries. The few monasteries left in the time of Alfred were clearly impoverished and in need of reform. In this dark period of Anglo-Saxon monasticism many made monastic vows, but these vows were understood not as the beginning of a life in a community under a common discipline (a life under the rule) but as an act of piety which may have involved little more than the decision to remain celibate. Even Alfred the Great had been ineffective in his effort to revive the regular life.

Thus the reform of monasticism in the tenth century by Dunstan, Æthelwold, and Oswold under the aegis of King Edgar could be called the reestablishment of monasticism. It was connected with the earlier age of Anglo-Saxon monasticism only sentimentally, insofar as it attempted to rival the achievements read about in Bede and visibly apparent in the monuments. It is at this point that Benedictinism in the strict sense was introduced in England.

The three great leaders were deeply influenced by a contemporary monastic reform movement on the Continent which is usually associated with the Benedictine abbey at Cluny, although it had many centers (of which Fleury was the most important for England) and took a number of slightly varied forms. The reform movement had two purposes. First, it sought to free the monasteries of the influence of lay founders and landlords who too often treated them as private property, interfered in the election of abbots, and allowed the *Rule* to be disregarded. The reformers on the Continent often followed the example of Cluny and secured independence by placing themselves under the patronage of the Popes; in England, for reasons of distance from Rome and because the kings took the side of the reformers against the landlords and lax monks, the patronage of the crown was sought. The second purpose of the movement, which is really inseparable from the first, was to restore a strict observance of the *Rule* as it was currently understood and as it had been amplified by Benedict of Aniane in the *Capitula* of Aachen. One further tendency derived from the effort to introduce pure

Benedictinism: an enlargement of the daily offices and, in general, an inclination to enrich the liturgical life of the monasteries. Because of this latter fact, the Cluniac movement has sometimes been treated as an almost purely liturgical reform, incidental though this aspect of its work was to the primary goals of the reformers.

The English monastic revival left as its primary documentary witness the *Regularis Concordia,* promulgated around 970 in order to secure uniformity of practice. The document and the meeting at which it was adopted were modeled on the *Capitula* of Benedict of Aniane and the synod of Aachen at which they were ratified in 817. If the *Regularis Concordia* differed significantly from the practices of reformed monasticism on the Continent, it did so in its attitude toward superior ecclesiastical and lay authority. Allusion has been made already to the relationship of monks and king in England; this is codified by the document. More significant, however, is the proviso in the Proem that, where the monastic community served as the *familia* or staff of a cathedral, the bishop should be elected by the monks and should continue to conform to the rule. On the Continent the desire to free the monasteries from the control of local bishops was as strong as the desire to be independent of lay magnates. But the leading figures of the Anglo-Saxon hierarchy were by the 970s the leaders of the monastic revival, and it seems clear that they wished to monasticize the entire church. At any rate, this and other provisions—such as the one which makes it clear that the laity attended Mass with the monks on Sundays and Feasts (chap. 1)—show that English monks shared the pastoral ministry with the bishops.

The last observation points to another alteration in practice: whereas the *Rule* (chap. 60) makes it clear that in the sixth century it was exceptional for monks to be priests as well, the *Regularis Concordia* expects that monks of the proper age will be in clerical orders. Monasticism was at first both a lay movement and an anticlerical one. Given Gregory the Great's innovative use of monks as missionaries, it seems clear that many Anglo-Saxon monks must have been in clerical orders by the seventh century. The revival seems to have restored this order of things, and it was obviously more and more exceptional for the monk not to have been in orders. The increased importance of the Mass in the life of the monastery (it is only quite incidentally mentioned in the *Rule*) also testifies to the clericalization implicit in the movement. There is provision for private Masses for the dead. The monks are expected to receive Communion daily and to make confession weekly.

Perhaps the spirit of the *Regularis Concordia* is best captured by a drawing in an eleventh-century manuscript of the document. Seated at the upper portion of the picture in chairs canopied by an arcade are a king, an archbishop, and a bishop (the latter two with nimbuses), all of whom clasp an unrolled scroll. This must represent the legislators responsible for the document: King Edgar; St. Dunstan, Archbishop of Canterbury; and St. Æthelwold, Bishop of Winchester. Below, a monk is kneeling and, looking up at the other figures, clasps another scroll which he is wrapping about himself like a girdle. English monasticism, the drawing declares, has prospered because it bound itself to the legislated wisdom of the monastic reformers and their royal patron.

Anglo-Saxon monasticism must, then, be considered in two distinct periods. The earlier, from the conversion to the coming of the Vikings, was a period of eclecticism insofar as customs were concerned, although there was always a tendency to look to Rome, whence Gregory's monastic missionaries had come, for guidance. To this period also belong the Saxons' missionaries to the Continent and the decisive role played by Anglo-Saxons in the development, among other things, of Carolingian monastic policy. The second period is that of the revival of monasticism after an almost total eclipse. It began about 940 and continued with remarkable vigor to the Norman Conquest. Part of what is generally called the "Cluniac" movement, the monastic revival set the standards of intellectual and religious life at the end of the Saxon age, and the men it produced counseled kings, wrote codes of law and treatises of theology, built churches, and made beautiful books. The "gathering of all the honey in one hive" by Edgar's monastic "bees" was an act immeasurably good for the religious and literary nourishment of Englishmen.

B. EDUCATION

The following passage is the introduction of a little tract by Bede called *De Schematibus* which, with its companion *De Tropis*, served as a textbook on figures of speech for Bede's students. Originally both were appended to a disquisition on Latin prosody:

It is quite usual to find that, for the sake of embellishment, word-order in written compositions is frequently fashioned in a figured manner different from that of ordinary speech. The grammarians use the Greek term "schema" for this practice, whereas we correctly label it a "manner," "form," or "figure," because through it speech is in some way clothed and adorned. Metaphorical language is also quite commonly found when, either from need or for adornment, a word's specific meaning is replaced by one similar but not proper to it. The Greeks pride themselves on having invented these figures or tropes. But, my beloved child, in order that you and all who wish to read this work may know that Holy Writ surpasses all other writings not merely in authority because it is divine, or in usefulness because it leads to eternal life, but also for its age and artistic composition, I have chosen to demonstrate by means of examples collected from Holy Writ that teachers of secular eloquence in any age have not been able to furnish us with any of these figures and tropes which did not first appear in Holy Writ.

In what follows Bede clearly intends to teach students in his monastery to write elegantly by imitating the figurative language of the Bible.

The fact that the monastic institutions almost singlehandedly kept alive classical learning in the Early Middle Ages is well known but frequently misunderstood. It might perhaps be approached first as a phenomenon analogous to that which caused the offspring of the Germanic peoples to preserve so tenaciously the memory and some of the customs and traditions of their pre-Christian ancestors. That is, the temper of the Early Middle Ages was profoundly conservative. One hardly ever tried consciously to create something new—although the history of the relationship of "Benedictinism" to the Rule of Benedict and of the evolution of the attitude of monasticism towards secular life demonstrates that change and development did occur, often without being recognized as such. One attempted to preserve, to pass on, to keep alive the learning of the past and to assure that what one asserted in writing was backed up by the similar or identical sentiments of predecessors in the intellectual tradition.

To put the matter another way, scholars had in the Early Middle Ages (often with good reason) an extremely modest view of their own intellectual capacities and an enormous respect for the authority of written records with some claim to antiquity and some pretense of having been written by a man noted for piety or wisdom or both. That which was old and was by a famous man and was widely admired was most likely to be true; and if one wanted to write something orthodox, he turned to the authorities and, as often as not, copied them out verbatim. A number of writers—Bede and Ælfric are good examples—were fairly careful to indicate their sources, but on the whole plagiarism was not recognized as a sin. It is for this reason, as Beryl Smalley has pointed out, that scholarship about the Early Middle Ages often consists primarily in the study of the sources of any given document. The scholar's reward comes from discovering that his author had a large library, or a small library of anthologized comments on his subject or perhaps that old sentiments have been put together so as to produce a new effect. Wherever he finds passages for which no source is identifiable, the student must at least leave open the possibility that, in fact, they are not original but that either the source has been lost or he has not looked diligently enough.

The matter can perhaps be stated most clearly in terms of a doctrine of authority. Every age has had some understanding of an authority or means of demonstrating the truth in intellectual or scholarly argument. In the modern world, the authority has tended to be personal experience—anything from a laboratory experiment to a personal revelation of religious truth (like the moment in which John Wesley's heart was "strangely warmed"). His job in communicating this truth to others is to demonstrate the universality of his own experience by producing for others (by repetition of the experiment or preaching in the two cases cited above) the same or a similar experience. In an earlier period, the Middle Ages and Renaissance, there were two correlative forms of authority. The first was the ideas of ancient writers, both secular and religious (indeed, pagan and Christian).

The second—and for the moment, more important—was logical demonstration. To be true an idea ought to have witness in ancient or classical "authorities," but it ought also to be susceptible to logical demonstration. The example of Anselm has already been mentioned in this connection in Chapter I. Even more audacious was Abelard, who collected in his *Sic et Non* (*Yes and No*) conflicting statements of theologians on a number of points. Often Abelard has been considered a modern skeptic and debunker. Actually, his purpose was probably to point out passages which required the attention of logically trained theologians if the whole body of theological thought was to assume the consistency and unity he believed ought to characterize the most sublime body of knowledge.

The approach of Anselm and Abelard was the fruit of an intellectual revolution, a key factor of which had been the revival of the discipline of logic, which had not been a salient feature of academic discipline in the Early Middle Ages. In that period, virtually the sole sort of authority was antiquity. That which was vouched for by the ancient writers was true; and, given the almost exclusively theological preoccupations of the intellectuals of the Early Middle Ages in England as on the Continent, the authorities which were used tended to be the Bible and the writings of the Fathers of the Church. The most prominent of the latter were Jerome, the translator of the Bible in the Vulgate Latin version; Augustine of Hippo, not so much as author of the *City of God* as of a number of biblical studies and sermons; Gregory the Great; and Ambrose of Milan. A rather latter-day figure was Isidore of Seville (*c.* 560–636), an encyclopedist or collector and collator of the sentiments of others, whose love for etymological analysis (often, to us, far-fetched) was particularly infectious. Bede, too, quickly assumed an equivalent sort of authority, which was a tribute to his remarkably wide reading, genuine powers of synthesis, and winsome Latin style. In more mundane affairs, such as dispute over the ownership of real property or monastic custom, documents of less ancient and exalted origin exercised comparable influence under this same general doctrine of authority.

One of the problems inherent in this heavy reliance on source materials as authorities for truth was that the authorities themselves sometimes disagreed. For some of the lesser theological writers of the period, this fact seems not to have been a problem, and mutually contradictory theological ideas were often put side by side in the same book. Some of the scholars of the monastic revival seem to have made an effort to avoid such contradictions; but, when the most important writer of this group, Ælfric of Eynsham, questioned his sources, his ground was usually that there was reason to doubt the authority of the book in question and not that the arguments the book made were inherently illogical and therefore unacceptable. It might be said, indeed, that one of the characteristics of early medieval intellectual work is that it is often a-logical or that assertions are frequently made and arguments can be developed without the kinds of logical ordering and deduction which are common later in the medieval period. To be without logic is not to be confused with being illogical. It is rather an implication of a situation in which truth is that which is vouched for and witnessed by authority. To restate the authorities is to state the truth; and the form of the statement—its development and logic—has nothing to do with its veracity. Good writers will try to make truth attractive; but the package has nothing to do with the value of its contents.

This fact may in part explain the narrative phenomenon in *Beowulf* which Klaeber called "lack of steady advance." The well-made plot, of which so many critics and students have wished the *Beowulf*-poet capable, is a logical device. But logic has little to do with the telling of the story of Beowulf, which the poet has on authority and recounts in a traditional manner. The poet and his audience were interested in what the tradition said about Beowulf and related matters, not in whether it is a logically coherent story after the manner of a modern historical novel.

Perhaps the matter of early medieval doctrine and practice concerning the nature of the truth can best be summed up by reference to the famous dictum of an early fifth-century monk, Vincent of Lerins: "In the catholic church itself especial care must be taken that we hold to that which has been believed everywhere, always, and by all men." Ecumenicity, antiquity, and consensus are the three rules or tests to which one subjects religious teaching in order to distinguish truth from heresy. The tests were applied throughout the Early Middle Ages. If the results were often patently unscientific, the fault may have lain less in the Vincentian rule itself than in the failure of the curricula of the early medieval schools to stress the discipline of logic which provides the skills necessary for application of the rule.

A good deal less than one would like is known about the forms taken by education in this period, but the general outlines are fairly clear. Benedict of Aniane attempted to remove monasticism from the business of education in order to keep it from contact with the world. But the Cluniac reformers and their Anglo-Saxon descendants, like the earlier monks, seem to have ignored this prohibition. At least, after the court school of Alfred, there is virtually no reference to secular schools in England; and it is clear that Ælfric in particular was concerned when he wrote the *Colloquy* and *Grammar* and *Glossary* to provide basic texts for monastic schools. The *Regularis Concordia* has a number of references to the regulations made for the boys' welfare within the monastic discipline. These include special provision for a visit to the latrine after the Night Office and regulations concerning the relationship of the boys, their master, and the monks, which seem to be designed both to preclude favoritism and to discourage homosexuality. It must be assumed that a number of these boys were in fact *oblates* dedicated to the monastery by their parents and training for the time of their full profession of the monastic life. But it can also be inferred that some persons who were not intended for monastic vows also received some or all of their educations from the monks. Of some such learned laymen, the lay patrons of Ælfric in particular, there is interesting record.

What exactly was taught is not so clear. In the sixth century, Cassiodorus, a Roman of senatorial rank like his younger contemporary Pope Gregory, having failed in an effort to found in Rome an institution for theological studies, established a monastery at Vivarium after his retirement from public life. This institution is often credited with having begun the tradition of scholarly monasticism in the West. Its inmates undertook both the study of theology and literature and the reproduction of manuscripts; and the founder in his *Institutes* was concerned not with the legislation of an ascetic discipline but with the definition and description of divine and secular letters.

Cassiodorus and others divided secular learning into seven disciplines, the Seven Liberal Arts: grammar, rhetoric, dialectic, arithmetic, music, geometry, and astronomy. These have often been subdivided, the literary studies of grammar, rhetoric, and dialectic being called the trivium and the four more advanced, scientific disciplines being designated as the quadrivium.

Whether Cassiodorus was widely known among early medieval educators in England is not certain, but his general approach to curricular structure (or the late classical approach) is thought to have been influential throughout the period. The trivium-quadrivium division seems to have been sustained, but it is unlikely that the full Cassiodorian curriculum was ever taught.

In theory, the disciplines were approached in sequence, but in practice they overlapped. The trivium was concerned with effective communication, and its disciplines had been developed in Greece and Rome not so much for writers as for statesmen or public speakers. It is a reflection of this fact that rhetoric dominated classical curricula from the Sophists to the fall of Rome and that a number of important early Christian figures (notably Augustine, who was a teacher of rhetoric before his conversion) were skilled rhetoricians. Grammar taught one both to write or speak correctly and to analyze and understand correctly the prose and verse utterances of others. Because it was usually taught by the use of models drawn from well-known books, the latter aspect of grammatical training was a natural step towards the former. Rhetoric, the next step, was the study of the art of persuasion. Indeed, it came to be the study of the figures of speech by which one made his argument both appealing and convincing. Since grammar included analysis of figures of speech and metrics, the pupil, after studying works like Bede's essay on schemes and tropes, had a fair knowledge of elementary rhetorical principles even if he did not go on to the advanced study. Dialectics or logic was the art of constructing arguments in issues under contention so that one's audience would be won to the correctness of one's views. Of the three disciplines of the trivium, grammar was clearly the most important for the Anglo-Saxons and for other early medieval educators. Indeed, it may be that the widespread knowledge of rhetorical figures among writers in both Old English and Latin (for which there is increasingly impressive evidence) was gained in the course of studies which did not go beyond the study of grammar, as it was conceived by Cassiodorus.

Some allusion was made to the rhetoricians; but there is no evidence that, except for the summary treatment in Book II of the *Etymologiae* of Isidore of Seville, rhetorical textbooks were widely known. The student who had mastered the *Ars Maior* of Donatus, Bede's *De Schematibus et Tropis,* or one of the many early medieval grammars had, however, a fairly good knowledge of the major rhetorical figures of speech.

The three standard works on grammar, all of which were used by Ælfric in his *Grammar,* were Donatus' *De Partibus Orationis Ars Minor* and *Ars Grammatica* (commonly called *Ars Maior),* and Priscian's *Institutio Grammatica,* written respectively in the fourth and sixth centuries. The *Ars Minor,* cast in the form of a dialogue and therefore useful for teaching and drilling beginners, deals very briefly with each of the eight parts of speech. The *Ars Maior* opens with a treatment of the voice as the medium of speech and considers, as aspects of voice, letters, syllables, metric feet, tone or accent, and punctuation marks. (Punctuation marks were regarded as guides for the oral reader, not as indications of transition between grammatical or syntactic units.) Next Donatus turned to a more leisurely examination of the eight parts of speech than he had allowed himself in the *Ars Minor.* He enumerated errors of speech and writing: barbarism (originally errors of pronunciation and spelling introduced by foreigners), solecism (misuse of the grammatical forms), and other "vices," treated together in a general chapter. Fourteen types of metaplasm (alterations of spelling for metrical or other reasons) were listed before the grammarian turned to his final topics: schemata and tropes. Schemata are arrangements of words in which the sense is not changed (e.g., *zeugma* is a scheme in which a single verb is related to several words in different ways). Tropes are figurative uses of words which change their meanings; among those types of tropes which remain familiar are metaphor, metonymy, epithet, synecdoche, hyperbole, and allegory. Priscian's *Institutio* is similar to the *Ars* of Donatus in purpose, but it is far more complete and more compendiously supplied with examples for the classical authors. Ælfric's *Grammar*, the oldest extant vernacular grammar of Latin, follows the pattern of Priscian and Donatus, but (because Ælfric was teaching Latin as a foreign language) it gives a fuller treatment of inflections and a far less compendious treatment of errors and rhetorical figures. This does not, however, mean that Ælfric was ignorant of the latter. The Anglo-Saxons and the Carolingians had produced a number of handbooks in the eighth and ninth centuries, some of which he surely knew.

The grammar books were not the only handbooks in use in the Anglo-Saxon schools. Treatises on Latin meters and the rhetorical figures taught in the grammar of Donatus were not uncommon. Colloquies or dialogues between masters and students, intended both for vocabulary drill and to teach the figures, were frequently produced. There were marginal *scholia* pointing out constructions and figures in numerous manuscripts of biblical books and Latin poetry. A number of *florilegia* or commonplace anthologies of quotations were assembled with an eye to illustrating the figures. Thus the educated Anglo-Saxon had a fairly extensive training in the art of writing and the use of figurative language, even though the curriculum probably did not often go beyond grammar to a treatment of the five divisions of rhetoric.

In terms of its effect on literature, the most obvious result of the teaching methods of textbooks like Bede's *De Schematibus* was highly conventional writing. The student learned by memorizing lists of figures and topics and by examining the Bible, poetry, and other writings as models of composition and effective rhetoric. When the student himself wrote, he was expected to reproduce both these conventions and authoritative ideas; and he was judged not in terms of his originality but in terms of his skill in employing the tried and true devices and themes. Often, when writers, like Aldhelm, were florid to the point of complete obscurity, it was not a matter of ignorance and inability to write clearly but of overzealous imitation of ornate stylistic models. At its best, however, the method produced simple, clear, and effectively persuasive writing.

The quadrivium must be dismissed rather quickly. Its disciplines did serve certain practical needs, however, which kept them alive for keeping accounts, making rather difficult computations to determine the date of Easter (which served to determine the date of the rest of the liturgical year and was computed on the basis of the Jewish lunar calendar rather than the classical solar calendar which had been adopted for general use by Christians), and arranging the musical services of the churches. Perhaps the most important evidences of the perseverance of the mathematical disciplines in the Early Middle Ages are the number of computational tables and directions for figuring the liturgical year and Bede's chronological studies, particularly the *De Temporum Ratione* which was later used by Ælfric in a similar work.

It should be clear from what has been said about the scholastic disciplines of the age that learning hardly survived for its own sake. As appropriated by the early medieval scholars, the classical fields of study were intensely practical. Those of the quadrivium served to plan and regulate the monastic day and year in an age when only the sun and stars were available for computing times and seasons. They served as necessary tools for carrying out the ordered discipline of worship which was a main reason for the existence of monasticism.

As for the trivium, its disciplines served two intensely practical ends in the eyes of most educators. They served, first, to preserve and pass on the record of religious revelation. Christianity depended from the start on the Scriptures and upon the interpretation of the Scriptures, in particular the voluminous writings of the Fathers which had been accepted as orthodox and against which all later commentary had to be tested for orthodoxy. Thus a purely oral religious tradition, such as evidently had sufficed for the Germanic pagans, was impossible for the Christians and (at the very least) a professional class which was literate and trained in the disciplines of interpretation had to be maintained.

The second purpose of education grew from the classical tradition of governance by written law. The church both assumed a role in civil administration, as the imperial government withered away, and developed a complex set of regulations and customs for its own functioning. Documents like the monastic rules and the *Regularis Concordia* reflect the use of learning for governing the church; and the church surely fostered the tendency to codify in writing Germanic customary or oral law in order to stabilize the general society in which it found itself.

Whenever learning did not serve these basic functions, its validity was questionable. But its utility and necessity were never doubted when it performed its defined functions with that same conservative spirit described at the beginning of this section. When King Alfred, outlining his educational program, said that the failure of his people to keep alive the educational tradition of the age of Bede and Alcuin was the direct cause of the divine retribution meted to the Anglo-Saxons by the Northmen, he was not being facetious. Religious and civil order in a Christian society depended upon the maintenance of a sound educational system.

C. Biblical Criticism

Medieval biblical exegesis resists adequate description. It must be read (preferably in large doses) if its spirit and method are to be understood. Unfortunately, little of it has been translated. The following text is presented only as an isolated example of early medieval exegesis. It is from Bede's commentary on Genesis. Like most exegetical commentaries, Bede's proceeds episodically, giving commentary on passage after passage so that it appears to the reader of the whole to be almost spasmodic and without artistic unity. Also, as in most similar works, the allegorical interpretations of Bede's commentaries are not original but are based upon traditional associations, some of which derive from the writings of the Fathers.

> Then God spoke to Noah, saying, "Go out of the ark, yourself and your wife, your sons and your sons' wives with them. Lead out with you the living beings which are with you of every kind, whether birds or beasts and all the reptiles which crawl upon the earth, and go out upon the earth. Increase and multiply and replenish it." And so Noah went out, and his sons, et cetera [Gen. 8:15-18]. By many and various means the mysteries of the church of Christ are repeated with the same frequently-iterated meaning. For the departure of Noah from the ark onto the earth which had been cleansed by the flood with those he had brought in with him, men and animals, is figuratively appropriate to that

time when the faithful—having been washed in the font of baptism in order to occupy themselves with good works in public (Noah being Christ the spiritual leader)—go forth and, ever increasing in spiritual virtues, increase and multiply. *Going*, he says, into the world, *teach all peoples, baptizing them in the name of the Father and the Son and the Holy Spirit* [Matt. 28:19]. Which is to say figuratively, "Bring every kind of living being into the ark for cleansing by water." And immediately he adds, *Teaching them to observe all of the things I have commanded you* [Matt. 28:20], as though to say typologically, "And having gone out of the ark after the flood, let all the living beings be led into the land which has reappeared and become verdant with new-sprung flowers, and there let them increase and multiply." And that they went out of the ark on the twenty-seventh day of the month, which number is the cube of three, as we have said before, signifies the perfection of the faith which is consecrated in baptism, because it cannot waver in any direction but always unsubdued and steadfast stands firm against all the stratagems of the devil. It is to be noted as according to the letter that those who went in on the seventeenth day of the second month and after a year disembarked on the twenty-seventh day of the same month were in the ark for an entire solar year. For example, if today, the kalends [first] of April, were the seventeenth day of the lunar month, the following year the day before the kalends of April would be the twenty-seventh of the lunar cycle, three hundred sixty-five days having passed and a solar year completed. Therefore, they were in the ark an entire year (that is, for how long the sun, having run through his course in the heavens for twelve solar months, should have illuminated all the regions of the world) so that, just as the water covering the earth drenched it, even so the sun cooperating with it (so to speak), and at the same time going around, radiated the earth with the light of its splendor. In the same manner the Lord is figuratively called both "the fountain of life" and "the sun of justice"—"fountain" because he regenerates, "sun" because he illuminates us, as the Psalmist says, *For with thee is the fountain of life, and in thy light we shall see light* [Psalm 35:10 (Vulgate)]. And Noah was in the ark for an entire solar year with those living beings and men who were being saved by the flood: for a year because God throughout all of this present age and throughout all the regions of the world both cleanses his church with the health-giving water of the bath and illuminates it with the grace of his spirit.

The Early Middle Ages inherited from the classical period a method of literary criticism or interpretation which often seems to the modern reader so strained and fanciful as to do violence to the rather straightforward biblical texts purportedly under examination. Yet the method of biblical exegesis and many of the apparently outlandish conclusions it reached derived from a serious intellectual tradition of the highest order, which requires some attention before the passage from Bede on Noah can be appreciated.

The medieval exegetical tradition had its roots in late Greek criticism of the epics of Homer. Hellenistic philosophy had developed a dualistic and negative view of the physical world as the place or condition in which man, originally a purely spiritual creature, lived entrapped by flesh. He either, according to the Stoics, suffered his state passively or, according to the followers of Plato, attempted by means of an education of the soul to achieve its restoration to the spiritual realm from which it had fallen. In either case, the flesh was both a trap and a distraction for man's spiritual being. The currency of this view made the activities of both gods and men in the *Iliad* and the *Odyssey* an embarrassment which was intolerable to the philosophers (and to ethnic pride), for at the same time Homer was universally regarded as the poet *par excellence*. Since on the surface the tales of Homer were so base and frivolous, it stood to reason that there was another level to their meaning. Thus it was sometimes maintained by Stoic critics that there must be such levels which served the truth as the philosophers understood it. Homer's tales were an allegory of dualistic philosophy; and the task of criticism, according to this rather special group of critics, was not simply to study the text, the prosody, and the narrative of the poems, but also to unveil the mysteries hidden to all but the initiates of philosophical truth.

This new method of literary criticism was first applied to biblical texts in Alexandria, the great center of Hellenistic intellectual life, by Philo (d. *c.* A.D. 50), who was a member of that city's large Jewish community. Cultivated Jews living in the Greek world found the crudity of the Books of Moses—which depicted God creating the world of flesh and finding it good, walking in the garden and making noise, appearing and speaking to man, concerned with the historical destiny of a people—as great an embarrassment as the philosophers found Homer. The adherent of the cult of such a God could not possibly gain a hearing in educated circles in the Hellenistic world. So Philo made of the Books of Moses an allegory of philosophical enlightenment or salvation and of Moses a new philosopher. Whether or not Philo exerted any influence on Christian exegesis is a disputed issue which need not be of concern here so long as the points are made that the method was classical and literary in origin and that the way to appropriating it to Biblical study was first pointed out by a Jew.

Another Jew, Paul, applied something like the method in writings which were to become authoritative for Christians. Paul attempted to explain the nature of the relationship between Old Testament events and persons and the Christian events of salvation. For him, Abraham's slave woman who bore him a son represented allegorically the terrestrial Jerusalem which is enslaved by the law and is the "mother" of the Jews; but Sarah, Abraham's wife and the mother of his heir Isaac, was the new Jerusalem which is free and is the "mother" of those who follow Christ. In addition to this kind of allegory, Paul employed typology, or the method of establishing relationships between historical personages and events. Adam, the one man through whom mankind came into a situation of bondage, is for Paul the type or anticipation or equivalent of Christ, the one man through whom mankind can emerge to a new freedom; and Christ's crucifixion and resurrection were anticipated typologically by the Passover, for both were acts which made possible a new, free life and established new communities (Jerusalem, the Church) of men in special relationship with God. The Epistle to the Hebrews demonstrates the same tendency among early Christian writers in a rather more advanced form.

Although some early Christian biblical scholars (the "Antiochene school") attempted to deal straightforwardly with the literal meaning of the Bible, by far the more important influence on medieval Christian scholarship was exercised by the "Alexandrian school," which attempted to expound the allegorical or "spiritual" as well as the literal or "historical" meaning of the scriptural texts. Among these, Origen (d. c. 254) was the greatest figure

Concerned, as Philo had been, to make doctrine comprehensible in the light of the teaching of the philosophers, Origen discerned levels of meaning in the biblical texts. He spoke about the levels of spiritual meaning in several ways. Often he said that Scripture had three levels of meaning, just as man was a tripartite being of body, soul, and spirit—a microcosmic organization which reflected the structure of the macrocosm. The historical or literal level was comparable to man's corporal nature; the psyche or soul had its counterpart in the moral or tropological meaning of Scripture; and the spiritual nature of man (that part which is closest to the divine) was reflected in the allegorical meaning of Holy Writ. Some passages—especially some which seem to convey no sensible or edifying message when read historically—might not have present in them all three levels of meaning. On occasion when the explication of the text was better served by the reversal, the allegorical sense was considered before the moral. In such cases, the moral (usually ascetic) sense grew from the allegorical and often a fourth level emerged in which Origen spoke of the implications for man of the attainment of his goal: communion with the godhead.

However, when Origen formally discussed the methodology of biblical criticism, he never mentioned more than three levels of meaning and usually set out the body-soul-spirit scheme. This had some influence, but it was the second arrangement, used by Origen in practice but ignored by him in theory, which was the more often imitated. It recommended itself to Gregory the Great and the monastic exegetes because it gave greater emphasis to the ascetic education of the soul and the vision of God, the goal of asceticism. The *lectio divina* or prescribed daily reading of the monks was intended as an exercise to nurture the ascetic or contemplative life; and an exegetical approach which found in the interpretation of Scripture means to purify and enlighten the soul fitted well into this regimen. Thus one comes to hear more often of four levels of scriptural meaning: historical, allegorical, moral or tropological, and anagogical.

Actually, however, it is fairly difficult in the Early Middle Ages to find passages which clearly spell out either the three- or the four-fold approach. Nevertheless, because each of the four senses or levels plays some role in the approach of early medieval men to the Bible, it is necessary to pause to speak of each and its significance. A classic example was given by John Cassian, the fifth-century apologist for monasticism in the West, in his *Conferences,* although the order—based on the first of Origen's systems—places the tropological sense last:

> One and the same Jerusalem can be taken in four senses: historically, as the city of the Jews; allegorically as the Church of Christ, anagogically as the heavenly city of God "which is the mother of us all," tropologically as the soul of man, which is frequently subject to praise or blame under this title.
>
> (XIV. 8)

Analysis of the historical sense of Scripture involved an examination of what was literally said. At its most basic level, this involved the grammatical examination of the structure of the passage under consideration and the following of the narrative thread. In treating some of the Psalms and poetic books like the Song of Solomon in which there was no obvious narrative or historically edifying description, the effort (beyond grammatical analysis) to expound the historical sense was often abandoned. The allegorical sense involved the recognition, particularly in treating passages from the Old Testament, of connections between events and personages of the Old and New Testaments, the former prefiguring the latter. Thus Jerusalem is the type of the church, Adam of Christ, and so forth. The anagogical sense was invariably eschatological in its implications. That is to say, it pointed to a connection between the biblical passage in question and the consummation of history, the Kingdom of God, the people of God, or the church perfected and in perfect communion with God. The moral or tropological sense—in the case of Jerusalem, fulminations like those of the prophets against the shortcomings of the city which was meant to stand in special and exemplary relationship with God—urged man to reform himself and to conform his will to the divine. When (as became more usual) the order ran allegory, tropology, anagogy, the moral teaching grew from the picture of the life as prefigured in the Old Testament and towards the picture of the fulfillment of the promise for which the church stood. The moral or tropological sense looked to the moral order of the world of the exegete and his audience and to man's longing for the perfected order of the Kingdom of God. The exegete admonished his audience in the light of present shortcomings to prepare themselves for the coming order. Scripture, it was believed, was the divinely inspired record of God's work for the salvation of mankind and the legislation under which man was to seek guidance. It must be edifying, therefore, in all its parts; and its meanings were not simply literal but multiple.

Medieval biblical exegesis is usually not congenial to modern readers unless examined in the context of the medieval understanding of history and eschatology. Medieval man saw all history as a unity, running according to the plan of God from the creation to the denouement of the Last Judgment and inauguration of the Kingdom. From the Fall to the Judgment, history was the story of man's efforts to attain salvation and of God's effort to bring man to salvation. The life of Christ, as the event in which God acted most decisively to achieve this end, was therefore the pivot of history; for only through Christ's effort was man's quest possible. Christ fulfilled the longings and efforts described in the Old Testament, and it was in the light of his achievement that later men attempted to prepare themselves for salvation. Because of this historical view, early medieval genealogists and historians customarily traced the roots of the persons and events they studied into the biblical period, thereby setting both past and present events into the only framework within which it was believed that they could be understood and evaluated.

The early medieval view of history had a wide perspective, looking forward to the Judgment and to the Kingdom as the fulfillment of history which ultimately and finally would vindicate or condemn the acts of men in history. Eschatology (literally, "the study of the last things") is a key to medieval thought, for men always reminded themselves that the measure of the success or failure of any action was not its immediate result but whether it would be acceptable to Christ the Judge when he returned at the end of historical time to begin the timeless and transformed Kingdom. The church was both the institution through which man was prepared for the eternal life of the Kingdom and, as a community, a kind of foretaste or analogue of what life would be like in the Kingdom. Man's effort was to win ultimate acquittal by the Judge and to become a member of the blessed society of the Jerusalem which is above.

Every passage of the Bible had to be seen in the light of this all-pervading view of history and eschatology. It had something to say about events in the biblical period, about some moment in the great drama of salvation. Each of these events was related to the events of the life of Christ or of the Church if it was allegorically or typologically understood. At the same time, it reflected upon the situation of man the reader or hearer of the Bible, for each man was involved in the same quest for salvation and could profit by the biblical examples, either negative or positive. And, therefore, since morality was always related to whether or not one was to be found acceptable by the Judge, it reflected analogously upon the eschatological picture—the picture of life as it was expected to be in the Kingdom of God. All the senses of Scripture—historical, allegorical, tropological or moral, and anagogical—were, then, integrally related to the medieval Christian understanding of man's destiny within and beyond history.

The earliest approaches to allegory as a means of understanding ancient literary texts—those of the commentaries on Homer, of Philo, Paul and Origen—were apologetic in purpose: they wanted to make sense of their documents in the light of an apparently uncongenial world picture. By the Early Middle Ages, the allegorical approach—articulated as an approach to literature by means of levels of meaning or spiritual senses—had been assimilated into a Christian world picture and made a tool for reading Scripture in the light of its implications for man's life and destiny.

It must be noted in passing that the allegorical sense (it is often and rather more accurately called *typological* or *figural*) characteristically elucidates the connection between historical events or persons or, at least, events or persons the commentator believed to be historical. It sets up a comparison between, say, Adam or Abraham as the *type* or *figure* of Christ. Greek and other classical allegorists aimed either at explaining the "deeper meanings" of the myths or at defending "the myth from charges of immorality or blasphemy." They moved from what most men in the late classical world regarded as fictions to abstract meanings. Christian typological or allegorical explication found relationships between historical persons, and it made further connections with the life of man in the present and with the Kingdom. Thus, by means of this web of relationships, it attempted to make the Bible immediately relevant to the student of its contents or to persons who heard in sermons and read in books the conclusions of such studies. Abraham is the type of Christ and by analogy is like the Kingdom of God. I (the reader or hearer of the Abraham story) look to Christ for the means of salvation and to the Kingdom for the fulfillment of salvation. So I am like Abraham, and there is a compelling moral lesson for me in his story, which helps to shape my life to the pattern set by Christ and to prepare me for the Kingdom. The historicity of Abraham served (in a way that is often difficult for us to appreciate) not to elongate the distance between Abraham and those who read of him in the Bible but to contract it, to make Abraham of immediate and existential importance. There were times when Christian allegorists tended to be more like the Greek because they dealt with abstractions more than historical realities. But on the whole the exegetes of the Early Middle Ages were both unequipped and unwilling to move from immediately relevant to more abstract and remote understandings of the nature of religious truth.

In the passage on Genesis at the beginning of this section, Bede places little emphasis on the historical sense. He accepts the historicity of the Noah story, regarding it as an account of an act of destruction and restoration only understandable and edifying in the light of the work of Christ for salvation, the destruction of the Last Times, and the Judgment which will issue in the inauguration of the Kingdom. Thus he is impelled to turn almost at once to the levels of allegory and anagogy. His concern with number symbolism, however, arises from the literal sense of the text; and his explanation of the significance of the date of the disembarkation is to be understood—as Bede himself stresses: *iuxta litteram*—as arising from the need for close and careful analysis of the text. Until one understands thoroughly the author's literal intention and grammatical craft, he cannot move on with assurance to the spiritual meanings of the text. Since the author is divinely inspired, no detail of the text is without purpose and significance. Elsewhere, Bede characteristically displays a fine feeling for the grammatical niceties of his text and points, for example, to the use of the imperfect tense as opposed to the perfect in cases where careless reading might lead to interpretation of an act as completed when, in fact, it was not.

The allegorical and tropological senses are so intertwined in the quotation from Bede that it is hard to decide which was intended to have priority. Indeed, the tropological interpretation is all-but-subsumed in the allegorical. It consists simply of the implication that Christians are expected to do good works and to convert others. Bede's primary concern is with the typological associations of the ark with the Church, of Noah with Christ, and of the experience of surviving the Flood with the experience of Christian baptism. By means of these identifications, he brings a remote, curious, and colorful tale into direct connection with Christian teaching and with the experience of his audience. If the ark is the Church, then churchmen must be vitally concerned with the ark story as a story about themselves.

The numbers mentioned by the author of Genesis suggest perfection to Bede, and the notion of perfection brings him to the anagogical level; for the Kingdom of God is the perfection of which the Church is a token and for which it waits in the world. The year Noah spent in the ark represents the millennium, and his disembarkation is, thus, analogous to the inauguration of the Kingdom.

Bede's explication of the Noah story is a good example of early medieval exegesis because of its imperfection. Rarely did the exegetes follow through the four steps systematically. Indeed, it is frequently difficult to know which of several variant systems or approaches to the multiple senses of the Scriptures is being followed, and individual authors often shifted their approaches. As W. F. Bolton puts it:

> Bede is a characteristic figure in the tradition: although systematic statements of the allegorical method abounded, the practice was almost always . . . pragmatic. There is no compulsion to link levels of meaning, and no prohibition from "mixing" them. In every instance the contingencies of spiritual need, rather than the rules of exegetical theory, guide his commentary.

After Bede, there were developments in biblical study, most of them based on a better understanding of the conventions and methods of patristic exegesis, but in essence the practice of scriptural explication remained unchanged. Miss Smalley has, however, suggested that at the time of the monastic reforms of the tenth century there was "a dramatic pause in the history of Bible studies" which is attributable to the increased interest of the monks in liturgy at the expense of the *lectio divina*. Monastic worship was enhanced by a new approach to music, by enrichment of the texts and actions of the services themselves, and (above all) by the appropriation of the understanding of the multi-layered sense of the Bible to the interpretation of the meaning of the liturgy. One suspects that the sermons of Ælfric may belong as much to this impetus as to the older tradition of exegesis as an exercise in contemplative discipline or to the tradition of homiletic explication. The study of the Bible was to be revived in the twelfth century and to be carried forward under the influence of the new passion for dialectics. It became, thereafter, a far more orderly academic discipline. Thus, as is the case with many other areas of endeavor, early medieval biblical study is to be seen as belonging to a distinct and clearly distinguishable period of literary and intellectual development.

One final word must be said: early medieval exegesis grew not only from the patristic tradition but also from the educational tradition. It was literary criticism—although criticism of a very special sort of text—which was designed both to expound the profundity of the passages under consideration and to move the audience. It was, in other words, ultimately rhetorical and intended to have an effect on the hearer, if it was cast in the form of a sermon, or the reader, if it was a commentary read by monks as a part of the ascetic discipline.

In this connection, modern students are usually directed to the *De Doctrina Christiana* of Augustine, a work whose title, it has been suggested, might be rendered, *"Exegetical Handbook, with a Guide to the Biblical Instruction of Christians."* Exaggerated and sometimes misguided claims have been made for the nature and influence of this work, and it may be best to approach the subject by means of Bede's *De Schematibus et Tropis*. In his discussion of tropes (figures of speech "in which a word, either from need or for the purpose of embellishment, is shifted from its proper meaning to one similar but not proper to it") Bede followed Donatus and others in listing allegory as one of several tropes with a number of subtypes (irony, antiphrasis, enigma, charientismos, paroemia, sarcasm, asteismos); but he departed from his sources in the excursus he allowed himself on the nature of allegory after he had listed the various types. He distinguished between "Factual Allegory" which arises from the typological relationships (for example, the two wives of Abraham as the two covenants) and "Verbal Allegory" which arises from the biblical authors' use of metaphoric and often obscure language (for example, the "shoot" from the "stock of Jesse" which "shall bear fruit," a passage which posits the rise of the Messiah from the house of David). In either case, allegorical meaning arises from the literal sense of the text and is likely to lead one on to tropological and anagogical implications. What this suggests is that the "allegorical method" of explication was not simply an exotic intellectual game. It was rather a means of getting at the meaning of a profound series of texts dealing with matters of the utmost importance. It both grew from the classical tradition of literary study and was assimilated into that very practical curriculum which was the chief heritage of the classical period in the Early Middle Ages. In Augustine's *De Doctrina Christiana*, it became a tool for expounding the Bible orally in sermons. The work of the former teacher of rhetoric provided an approach to the problem of finding a style sublime enough to be suitable to the most elevated subject matter and yet simple enough to instruct and move the least sophisticated in the congregation. In Bede, the allegorical method is assimilated unobtrusively into a handbook for students (itself an appendix to an introduction to the study of Latin metrics) who are themselves beginning to learn the art of analyzing and interpreting literature. They will master the tropes or literary devices as well as the traditional typological associations before they themselves put the method to work either as preachers or as monks meditating on Scripture as a part of the discipline of contemplation.

D. MONASTICISM, EDUCATION, EXEGESIS, AND POETRY

It is time now to apply the topics considered in this chapter to the interpretation of an Old English poem. The following verses are the fifth division of a poem variously called *The Old English Advent* and *Christ I*. They are a meditation on a Latin antiphon ("O Orient, splendor of the eternal light and sun of justice: come and enlighten those who sit in darkness and in the shadow of death.") which was sung before and after the Magnificat (Luke 1:46–55) at the office of Vespers during Advent. The poem survives in the Exeter Book, an anthology of Old English poetry put together in the latter half of the tenth century and left to the library at Exeter by Leofric, bishop of Exeter, at his death in 1072. Dates as early as about 800 have been offered for its composition. The *Advent* was composed according to the standard rules of Germanic versification as they were employed by the Anglo-Saxons; but its subject matter, both in terms of source and development depends upon a complex and sophisticated Christian tradition.

Oh Morning Star, brightest of messengers
Sent to this earth, and to men, truest   105
Radiance of the eternal Sun, clear
And glorious beyond all stars, in every
Season glowing with Your own light!
God Himself brought You forth,
God creating God, Heaven's   110
Glory knowing no beginning. Now
God's other creation calls to You, needing You,
Hoping You will hear us, send us Your holy
Light, praying for Your shining truth
To burn where darkness has covered us over,   115
Here in our long night, crouching
In unending blackness, wrapped in our sins,
Enduring the evil shadows of death.
Now, hopeful, we trust in Your healing
Word, brought us from God, Word   120
Which was spoken in the beginning, which came from God
And itself was eternal God, Word
Which turned into sinless flesh, when the Virgin
Bore our salvation. God walked among us,
Pure, the Almighty's Son and the Son   125
Of Man the same, came to our misery
And sorrow, and was joy. We thank You, Lord
Of victory, for ever and ever, grateful for
Your grace in taking our flesh for our sake.

Advent, which has twelve divisions, consists chiefly of reflections upon antiphons sung at Vespers during Advent in conjunction with the Magnificat, the hymn recited by the Virgin in response to the announcement that she is to bear the Messiah. The poem is incomplete; but it must have presented the seven "Great O" antiphons in combination with others and in conjunction with various kinds of meditation in an ensemble which is not exactly duplicated in medieval liturgical texts and manuals. Nevertheless, it is clear that the background of the poem is liturgical and that the poet has applied the exegetical method to the interpretation of the liturgical texts. This in itself is moderately surprising and helps to date the poem, because, although Alcuin is credited with the first application of allegory to the liturgy in the West, the method was not systematically applied before the work of Amalarius of Metz (d. *c.* 850). After Amalarius' work, at first thought excessively allegorical, had taken hold, it became usual to seek symbolic justification not only for the words of the rites of the Church but also for every gesture of the participants. (It is not surprising that the first traces of liturgical drama are found in this milieu; and Division VII of *Advent* is a dialogue between Joseph and the Virgin which anticipates later dramatic conventions.) Since the state of Anglo-Saxon monasticism was so low in the ninth century, it is difficult to imagine that *Advent* could have been composed before the time of the monastic revival of around 940, at which time a concerted effort was made to enrich the liturgy in England.

Among the works of Amalarius of Metz is a commentary on the Antiphonary or book of antiphon texts, a version of which he himself had edited. In the chapter which treats the "antiphons which begin with O," Amalarius suggests that "O" imparts suitably the sense of wonder felt by those who contemplate the coming of Christ, and he relates the series of antiphons to the seven gifts of the Holy Spirit. Although Amalarius' comments on the "O Oriens" (the source of *Advent,* Division V) were probably not known to the poet, they are worth quoting as an example of the allegorizers' approach to liturgical texts:

> Beyond doubt the fifth [antiphon] stands in awe of the unaccustomed rising [of Christ, the sun], which is not (as you would expect) changed according to the custom of normal temporal

changes, but is unchanged; the sun of this rising illuminates not only the eyes of the body but also the mind. For justice pertains to the sight of the mind. This antiphon corresponds with the fifth stage of spiritual knowledge. For spiritual knowledge, which is in Christ, knows what he punishes compassionately and what he pardons compassionately. For the rising of knowledge, which is rooted in charity, is Christ. It is the work of justice alone to render knowledgeable the eyes of the mind when they gaze upon it.

Amalarius gives equal weight to the sun as the source of illumination and of justice and links the two, since the perception of divine justice is an aspect of spiritual illumination. His interpretation, here as with the rest of the series of antiphons, is designed to stress the connection of liturgical devotion with the contemplative discipline of monks, and it achieves a rich typological interpretation of the text. A similar congeries of ideas—with the added notion of regeneration by water—was evoked by Bede in the passage quoted above from his commentary on Genesis 8 as a typological implication of his observation that Noah was in the ark for an entire solar year.

Unlike Amalarius, the Old English poet seems to have ignored the theme of justice in the antiphon, except for his use of *soðfæsta*, "just," "righteous" (line 106; in the translation, "truest," line 105), which weakens the sense of the Latin *sol iustitiae*, "sun of justice." The motif may, however, be implicit in such expressions as *geomrum to geoce*, "as succor for the mournful" (line 124; in the translation, "our salvation"), since the phrase hints the kind of merciful judgment of which Amalarius speaks. Whatever the case, it is clear that the poet and the tradition of interpretation he followed chose rather to stress the Christological significance of the antiphon.

It has recently been claimed that Division V reflects the refutation of the Arian heresy, in which it had been argued that the Son was not coeternal with the Father. A favorite answer to Arianism employed the analogy of the inseparability of the sun from its light to demonstrate the inseparability of the Father and the Son. It is also possible that the images may have been revived in the controversy between Carolingian and Spanish theologians which arose over the use by the latter of the legal image of adoption to explain the relationship of Father and Son—an error which grew from a phrase in the Mozarabic liturgy. At any rate, phrases reflecting disputes over heresies tended to find their way into liturgical texts, once the issues had been settled, in order to discourage their cropping up again, and some of the poet's most important phrases—notably *god of gode* (line 109; in the translation, "God creating God," line 110)—reflect this kind of association. Alcuin's effort to introduce the recitation of the anti-Arian Nicene Creed into the Mass was probably a part of his program to assure that such errors as Adoptionism could not arise again so easily.

The exact doctrinal and exegetical backgrounds of the *Advent*, Division V, remain obscure, and any connections with Amalarius or with Adoptionism are probably fairly remote. Nevertheless, it is clear that the verses were conceived within the general framework established by the teaching of grammar in the schools and the application of the exegetical method. It will be remembered that Bede distinguished between typological or "factual" allegory, based on identification of an Old Testament person or place (as Jerusalem, in Division III) with Christ or the Church, and "verbal" allegory in which Christ or the Church is represented metaphorically. The basic light image of the invocation of the "O Oriens" antiphon falls clearly into the latter category. A student analyzing the text with the aid of Bede's handbook might further have recognized the verbal allegory of Division V as enigma, a subtype of the figure or trope of allegory "in which the meaning of a statement is hidden by the use of obscure analogies." All of the terms by which Christ is addressed in the first five lines would fit into that category. The terms of the next lines—*god of gode, sunu soþan fæder* (both credal formulas; the latter, meaning "son of the true father," is omitted in the quoted translation)—are, however, examples of antonomasia or "the use of an epithet in place of a proper name."

Beside the tropes or figures in which the meaning of words is shifted, *Advent*, Division V, uses schemata or special arrangements of words which were recognized in the grammatical tradition. The first five lines, for example, are representative of prolepsis, "anticipating or taking up in advance" before the subject of the trope is identified. The light images of these lines clearly involve an enigma, the subject of which is only identified with the antonomasia for Christ in line 109. A number of other schemata and tropes might be identified, but enough had been said to make the point that Anglo-Saxon students were exposed to close study of figurative, poetic diction and that their Old English poetry employs such diction as well as conventional, native locutions and figures.

More important, however, is the fact that Bede recognized the connection between the grammatical trope of allegory and the exegetical method and discussed the manner in which an allegorical trope can lead to reflection on tropological or moral and anagogical meanings as well as upon the historical referent and the antetype of Christ or the Church to which the historical points. The Old English meditation on the antiphon has, of course, no historical referent and, therefore, is an example of a case in which there is no literal meaning. But the rising sun image is rooted in common biblical symbolism, and its use is thus justified both by tradition and authority. The light image refers, allegorically, to the Incarnation or coming of God in Christ into the world, born of the Virgin. The petition of the antiphon asks Christ to come to those who are presently in darkness, but the *Advent* poet changes the tense to the past in lines 115b–118. The grammatical shift underlines his notion that the light allegorically points to the past or historical coming of Christ as it was described in the New Testament.

The *Advent* poet does not at this point in his sequence explicitly proceed to consideration of tropological and anagogical meanings. Since the twelve divisions of his work must be understood as an artistic whole, however, it can be argued that both meanings are expressed elsewhere and are implicit here. One of the themes of the poem is spiritual exile, which is itself often a metaphor for the contemplative aspect of monastic life in Old English poetry. The goal of contemplation is spiritual illumination, which can only be achieved by receiving or appropriating the light of Christ. Tropologically, then, the poem implies that illumination is only available to the contemplative by means of the presence in himself of Christ. And, of course, anagogically the Kingdom is a kingdom of light, of perfected vision of the Godhead.

Approached for the first time, *Advent*, Division V, appears to be a simple and moving hymn of thanksgiving for the coming of Christ, the Light, into the world. It is that, of course; but it is also a poem with complex and sophisticated intellectual presuppositions. Thus the experience of the reader is considerably enriched if he has some knowledge of the monastic, educational, and exegetical factors which are part of its background.

IV. Man and His World
in Anglo-Saxon England

INCE THE RISE OF HISTORICISM IN THE NINETEENTH
century, historical study has too often been intrigued with the
notion that ideas and institutions emerge in ways which can be
detailed by the application of historical "laws" to whatever
evidence is available. These "laws" may be devised in the light
of a number of ideological foundations, of which Hegelian-
Marxist dialectic, Darwinian evolution, and the liberal idea of
progress are the most famous and influential. Not a few historians of Anglo-Saxon England have imposed the Hegelian pattern upon early English history. The Anglo-Saxons in their
original, Germanic state (thesis) confronted a totally alien, Latin-
Christian culture (antithesis); and after a period of conflict
caused by the exclusivism of the two approaches, a compromise
was reached in which the two were more-or-less harmonized
(synthesis).

The danger of this approach (as with the other sets of prop-
ositions concerning the workings of history) is that it is too
schematic, too neat to explain the facts which are available to
us. Furthermore, it tempts the historian to overweigh the element he personally most favors. If he sees in Germanicism a
kind of ideal and free (albeit primitive) society, he will attempt
to attribute to the Germanic strain all those traits of Anglo-
Saxon society which he finds most attractive. If he believes
that Christianity is the source of all that has been good and
beneficial in the Western tradition, he will try to show that
Christian and classical ideals overcame the native barbarism. The

results are an unedifying feud between the Germanizers and the Christianizers (not to mention the Celticizers) and studies which are not so much concerned with culture as it existed as with the sources of the culture. This is not to denigrate the utility and necessity of the study of the sources of culture but to urge that we must be concerned primarily to study literature within the actual context in and for which it was written and read.

The two preceding divisions of this volume have considered the chief strands of the literary culture of the Old English period —the Germanic and the Christian—in isolation from each other. The following sections will deal with attitudes and institutions which resulted from the meeting of the two as they are reflected by literature written or read in the period from Alfred the Great to the Conquest. No consistent effort will be made to isolate elements as deriving from the Germanic or the Christian heritage. Since the subject of this book is the presuppositions of the late Old English reading public, my concern has been to describe aspects of the culture of the literary audience as it is verified by the documents rather than the exact chains of influence by which the characteristic traits of that culture came into being.

A. Man and the Cosmos

Those who have read the background studies of Middle English and English Renaissance literature by C. S. Lewis and E. M. W. Tillyard will remember that a great deal of attention is given to cosmology, or man's picture of the nature and structure of his universe. Such ideas—and, certainly, the general Ptolemaic schema—are implicit as well in the Early Middle Ages, if only as a part of the lore inherited from late classicism. In such works as Bede's *De Temporum Ratione*, his other chronological studies, and Ælfric's Old English adaptation of Bede *(De Temporibus Anni)* much of this same information was available throughout the period. A number of books—especially calendars —contained charts reflecting cosmological notions and their astronomical ramifications. Occasionally, one comes across a manuscript drawing of the creation which also reflects these generally accepted ideas, sometimes connecting them with the theme of "the Spirit of God brooding on the waters" by using seven spheres to frame the illustration of the biblical verse. The *Chroni-*

cle notes the appearance of Halley's comet ("a sign in the skies such as had never been seen before") in 1066.

But such allusions to cosmological and astrological notions are far less common in Old English literature and less important for the interpretation of the writings than they are in the works of Chaucer or Shakespeare and their contemporaries. Often it is enough simply to hint at the existence of a multi-leveled universe. So, for example, the dreamer in the initial description of his vision in *The Dream of the Rood* speaks of the creatures which kept watch over the cross:

> Many bands of angels kept watch there, fair by eternal decree; surely [the cross in the vision] was not the gallows of a criminal, but holy spirits, men on earth, and all this glorious creation kept watch over it there.

(lines 9b–12)

The poet must have had in mind the kind of cosmic stratification represented in many manuscript illuminations in which zones —all transcended by the central image of Christ or the cross which unites heaven and earth—were devoted to various classes of creatures: angels at the top, holy spirits, men. By "all this glorious creation" the poet may either mean animal nature as the level of created being below man, or may intend a summary reference to the three classes already mentioned. However the poet intended the reader to picture the gems at the base of the cross in lines 7b–8a, his expression, "at the earth's surface," contributed to the general cosmological effect of the vision. This sort of cosmological allusion, which assumes a hierarchy of being in the most general way, is more typical of the spirit of Old English poetry than, say, Chaucer's carefully explicit statement at the end of *Troilus and Criseyde* that the hero ascended after his death to the eighth (or, in some manuscripts, seventh) sphere of the heavens or the care he has taken to mention the signs of the zodiac under which the characters in *The Canterbury Tales* were born.

The reasons for this apparent lack of concern for cosmological detail may be approached by means of an analysis of King Alfred's famous adaptation of Boethius' image of the orbiting spheres in *The Consolation of Philosophy*. First, we must look at the passage in Boethius' version:

> It follows then, that everything which is subject to Fate is

also subject to Providence, and that Fate itself is also subject to Providence.

Some things, however, which are subject to Providence are above the force of Fate and ungoverned by it. Consider the example of a number of spheres in orbit around the same central point: the innermost moves toward the simplicity of the center and becomes a kind of hinge about which the outer spheres circle; whereas the outermost, whirling in a wider orbit, tends to increase its orbit in space the farther it moves from the indivisible midpoint of the center. If, however, it is connected to the center, it is confined by the simplicity of the center and no longer tends to stray into space. In like manner, whatever strays farthest from the divine mind is most entangled in the nets of Fate; conversely, the freer a thing is from Fate, the nearer it approaches the center of all things. And if it adheres firmly to the divine mind, it is free from motion and overcomes the necessity of Fate. Therefore, the changing course of Fate is to the simple stability of Providence as reasoning is to intellect, as that which is generated is to that which *is,* as time is to eternity, as a circle to its center. Fate moves the heavens and the stars, governs the elements in their mixture, and transforms them by mutual change; it renews all things that are born and die by the reproduction of similar offspring and seeds. This same power binds the actions and fortunes of men in an unbreakable chain of causes and, since these causes have their origins in an unchangeable Providence, they too must necessarily be unchangeable. In this way things are governed perfectly when the simplicity residing in the divine mind produces an unchangeable order of causes. This order, by its own unchanging nature, controls mutable things which otherwise would be disordered and confused.

Therefore, even though things may seem confused and discordant to you, because you cannot discern the order that governs them, nevertheless everything is governed by its own proper order directing all things toward the good. Nothing is done for the sake of evil, even by wicked men who, as I have proved, are actually seeking the good when they are perverted by wretched error, since the order which flows from the center of the highest good does not turn anyone aside from his original course.

(IV. Pr. 6. 14–22)

Anicius Manlius Severinus Boethius (d. 524) is one of the most remarkable figures in Western intellectual history. One of the

last Westerners to have a sound knowledge of Greek and to know
both Plato and Aristotle in the original, Boethius would be important if the only surviving works were his logical treatises and
commentaries; for it was by means of these that the way to the
study of dialectics was reopened for the High Middle Ages. But
Boethius was a man of affairs as well, a Roman Senator and
sometime Consul; and it was apparently for his defense of the
prerogatives of the Senate that he was imprisoned and executed
under a charge of treason. During his imprisonment, he wrote
his great dialogue, *The Consolation,* a moving discussion between
himself and a feminine personification of philosophy of the nature
of true happiness and its relation to ill-fortune. Boethius was,
incidentally, a Christian and the occasional author of theological
tracts; but *Consolation,* devoid of specific Christian allusion, is an
essay on philosophical ethics in the Neoplatonic tradition.

The passage quoted above is typical of *The Consolation* in its
clear (and, therefore, "popular") presentation of Neoplatonic
concepts in idiomatic and yet rigorously logical form. Several
characteristics of the passage must be pointed out if we are to
understand the nature of the changes wrought by Alfred. As is
evident upon rereading, it is closely and rigorously argued; in fact,
it is basically a syllogism expanded by use of analogy without
any loss of coherence or economy.

Basic, as everywhere in the work of Boethius, is the idea that
God (or here, Providence) is eternal and, therefore, exists outside
of time so that all things are simultaneously present to him. God
sees as present the outcome of events which to man are sequen-
tial; and since he wills only the good, the outcome is good. To
man in time, of course, the outcome is not discernible and temporary reverses appear to be the workings of senseless Fate. The
only way man can free himself from the workings of Fate is
intellectual: he must understand what Philosophy can teach him
about the superiority of Providence to Fate and, by means of
understanding, be enabled to suffer Fate by knowing that the end
of events will be good. The problem of evil has not so much an
ethical solution as a metaphysical one: if one understands the
relationship of the eternal or timeless realm of being to the tem-
poral realm, he understands that evil is nonexistent. Things only

appear to be evil or Fate-controlled because of the limitations placed upon man's understanding by time.

The simile of the spheres, based on astronomy and geometry, is thus a logical analogy by which Boethius both illustrates and proves his point. The central point about which spheres orbit is stable and thus timeless, since mutability is the chief characteristic of being in time. The farther the sphere is from the center, the faster it moves and the greater its change. Fate can be said to be the laws which govern change; but those laws have their origin in the stable center and are therefore always working towards a rational, orderly end, in accordance with the will of the eternal being which is not subject to change.

Consider now the adaptation of the same passage by King Alfred:

> Certain things, then, in this world are subject to fate, some are not at all subject to it; but fate and all the things which are subject to it are also subject to divine providence. In this connection, I can tell you a parable so that you may more clearly understand which men are subject to fate and which are not. All this mutable and moving creation moves about the immutable God, steadfast and undivided; he rules all creatures which he designed in the beginning and still controls.
>
> Just as the axle of a wagon moves the wheel and the axle itself remains motionless and yet bears the entire wagon and controls all of its motion—the wheel moves about and the hub of the wheel, closest to the axle, travels much more steadily and more freely than the rim does—so the axle is the highest good, which we call God, and the best men travel closest to God like the hub which is closest to the axle; and middling men are like the spokes. For the one end of each spoke is attached to the hub and the other to the rim. Middling men are like that: one moment he considers this earthly life, the next the divine—as though he were looking with one eye to heaven and with the other to earth. As a spoke sticks one end in the rim and the other in the hub, midway it is equally near to both, though one end is attached to the hub and the other to the rim; so middling men are on the middle of the spoke, the better close to the hub and the basest to the rim. Nevertheless, they are fastened to the hub and the hub to the axle. The rims cling to the spokes although they are rolling entirely on the earth—so the basest men cling to the middling and

the middling to the best and the best to God. Although the basest direct all their love to this world, they cannot remain in it, nor does it avail them anything if they are not at all attached to God, any more than the rims of the wheel can be on the journey if they are not attached to the spokes and the spokes to the axle. The rims are farthest from the axle, thus they travel very unstably. The hub is nearest the axle and therefore goes with the greatest stability. So do the best men; as they place their love closer to God and more greatly despise earthly things, so they are more carefree and consider less how fate should vary or what it should bring. So the hub is just as sound, no matter where the rims rest and although it is somewhat separated from the axle. By this you can understand that the wagon is the more sound the less it is separated from the axle; and so men who are fixed to God are most untroubled concerning either the hardship of this life or the life to come; but the more they are separated from God the more they are troubled and afflicted both in mind and body.

So it is that what we call fate in connection with divine providence is like reflection and wisdom in comparison with perfect understanding or transitory things in comparison with eternal or the wheel in comparison with the axle; and therefore the axle controls the entire wagon. So does divine forethought; it governs the firmament and the heavenly bodies, and causes the earth to be still, and regulates the four elements (that is, water, earth, fire, and air). Now it reconciles and creates; at other times it deprives of form and brings forth in another form, and then renews, and brings forth all fruit, and again conceals and hides when it has grown old and withered, and afterwards renews and reveals as it wills. Some sages, however, say that fate controls both the prosperity and the misfortunes of every man. I say, as all Christian men say, that divine predestination controls it and not fate; and I know that it judges everything correctly, though unwise men think not. They think that anything is good which accomplishes their will; it is no wonder, for they are blind with the darkness of their sins. But divine providence understands it all very correctly, though we think on account of our foolishness that it goes wrongly because we cannot understand it rightly. He judges everything very justly even though at times we do not think so.

All men, whether good or evil, search for the greatest good, but the evil cannot come to the high roof of all good things for this reason: that they do not search for it correctly.

(XXXIX. 6–9)

To put the matter in the simplest terms: whereas Boethius approaches the problem of fate metaphysically, Alfred approaches it morally. For the one the problem is right understanding of the order of the cosmos, for the other correct orientation of the human will. Boethius uses the image of the orbiting spheres as a passing illustration of the relationship of providence to fate and of eternity to time. Alfred expands on the image so that it becomes an allegory of Christian life: one chooses to get on the wagon wheel; and, by the nature of his Christian commitment, one determines his own place on the hub or spokes or rim. Fate, therefore, is not a matter of apparent absurdity which becomes intelligible only when one understands that for God all events are present because the godhead exists outside of time. It is rather the consequence of the risk one takes by increasing the distance between himself (or his will) and the divine axle. The farther one is from the right-mindedness of God, the more mobile or mutable or unstable he is and the more subject to disaster.

In a very general way, Alfred is appropriating one strand of the Neoplatonic influence on early medieval Christian thought, namely the understanding of the ascetics that the closer the orientation of the will to God (and the farther the will from worldly distractions) the surer man is of salvation. But, like most other Christian moralists of his time, he discards the metaphysical foundation of Neoplatonic ethics in favor of a far more active and practical view of life. What happens to Boethius' Neoplatonic metaphysics in the hands of Alfred is comparable to what happened to Augustine's doctrine of predestination in the hands of most of the Western theologians, who were unwilling to sacrifice the freedom of the will and, therefore, the urgency of moral imperatives. It was for Alfred and for most contemporary thinkers imperative for men to do well in the world against all-but-overwhelming forces of evil, or even forces of simple ignorance and sloth. This belief led Alfred, he tells us in the Preface to his version of Gregory the Great's *Pastoral Care*, to undertake the translation of key books from Latin into Old English. Man must work to achieve these goals, which are sanctioned by God; he must be free to determine to act rightly, and he is fully responsible if he fails to do so.

Another, and perhaps the most accurate, way of stating the situation would be to say that Alfred's thought, like early medieval thought in general, was eschatological whereas Boethius' was teleological. Alfred takes as his basic presupposition the Christian view of history as a series of divine acts designed to redeem man and of human acts of failure to respond to the divine initiative. With Orosius (who had believed himself to be working out the implications of the view of history expressed in the earlier books of Augustine's *City of God*), he saw man's reverses as judgments upon man's failures. Individually and collectively the goal of man was to be found acceptable at the final judgment; and this meant that his good works in the world and his good intentions must outweigh his unacceptable works and thoughts. The expectation of judgment and the consequent sense of the moral urgency of the present life were postulates which informed almost every section of Alfred's Boethius and subtly motivated most of the alterations. For Boethius, however, the problem was to bring an innocent man to an understanding that evil is nonexistent and that, therefore, the suffering of the innocent in this world is only a temporary inconvenience. Although it does not necessarily preclude lessons concerning moral conduct, the primary effect of such knowledge is not to bring man to terms with his life but to enable him to endure it.

The evidence of the early medieval commentaries on Boethius shows that Alfred's version (although hardly a slavish adaptation of any known commentary) moves in the same general direction as the interpretations of his contemporaries. The notion that the best men are nearest to God and, therefore, most stable was applied by at least one other early medieval commentator to the Boethian image of the spheres in orbit; and this kind of alteration goes hand in hand with the general tendency of the commentators to make Boethius more explicitly Christian or theological at the expense of his metaphysical and logical subtlety. In this regard Alfred does not go so far as many of the commentators but is content to deal with Boethius' text fairly much as it stands in the light of his own Gregorian-Orosian conception of God and of the meaning of life in the historical world.

One final, general comment needs to be made about Alfred's approach to the image of the spheres in orbit. It is that the logical structure of the original has been undermined as well as its intellectual or metaphysical structure. A number of arguments has been offered in explanation of this fact, ranging from the king's naïvete to the limitations of Old English as a vehicle for logical argument. Given the early medieval curriculum, it should be clear that the failure is not surprising. Alfred was simply unequipped by his training to recognize the dialectical fashioning of Boethius' work. He aimed at clarification by means of something akin to explication and of repetition with variation. His sentences are paratactic, or made up of loosely connected coordinate clauses; Boethius' logic is reinforced by hypotaxis, the careful arrangement of clauses in dependent relationships. At moments, Alfred seems to strive for rhetorical effects and consciously to employ alliteration so as to move his audience to assent by aural rather than logical means:

> and tidreð ælc tudor,
> and hi eft gehyt and gehelt
>> þonne hit forealdod bið and forsearod,
> and eft geewð and geedniwað
>> þonne þonne he wile.

It may appear to the reader that we have strayed rather far from the subject of Anglo-Saxon cosmological belief, but it is important to set out these considerations in order to make the point that, although they accepted the cosmological tradition on authority, the Old English writers were not interested in the same implications of cosmology as the authors of the tradition and rarely stopped to treat it exhaustively or systematically. In the present case, although Alfred inflates a cosmological image in his source, he moves away from the metaphysical and epistemological implications of the image as it was presented in Boethius toward a moralistic, this-worldly application.

The same tendency is evident, though less markedly so, in his adaptations of the Meters or poems which precede and follow this passage. Meters 5 and 6 of Book IV of *The Consolation of Philosophy* are both hymns about the divine order which controls the universe. The movements of the heavenly bodies are a mystery to the uninformed, but to the philosopher they reveal the laws of nature: "All sudden and rare events bewilder the unstable and uninformed. But if the cloudy error of ignorance is swept away, such things will seem strange no longer." Boethius asserts that orderly change—the moving of the planets or the alternation of seasons—governs the cosmos. God controls all these movements and knows their purpose and outcome: "This is the common bond of love by which all things seek to be held to the goal of good. Only thus can things endure: drawn by love they turn again to the Cause which gave them being."

Alfred did not deal quite so radically with these cosmological Meters as he did with the prose portions of *The Consolation*. He first paraphrased them in prose and then he (or, perhaps, a follower) worked from the Old English prose to develop a poetic translation. In the course of this process one can see the same kinds of development already noted in the adaptation of the wheel image. In the Old English prose the idea of seeking "to be held to the goal of good" is expanded, made active, and treated in terms of the service done God by his creatures: "that they should serve such a lord, and they rejoice that he controls them." They would not exist, Alfred concludes, had the creator not made them, so their service is natural. In the verse treatment, the adapter goes back to the preceding sentence of the Latin, which states that without God to sustain them all creatures would lapse into non-being. By joining this idea to the idea of service to God as a loving response to the creator, the writer of the verse paraphrase makes the continued existence of creatures conditional on their loving service to the creator. The movement in Alfred, in other words, is always toward the moral obligation of man to respond to the relationship between God and himself, while in Boethius the emphasis is on the orderly functioning (independent of man's response) of a universe governed by a God for whom all things are present.

Alfred, and with him his early medieval contemporaries, adopted the Neoplatonic cosmology. The earth is the center of the universe, he says; therefore it is the stable body about which the heavenly bodies turn. Its stability is a gift of the divine forethought or Providence, and this same divine force regulates the rotations of the other bodies. The mind or intelligence which controls the universe controls as well all other things in it: the elements (the balance of which allows for the proper functioning of the natural law), the seasons with their cycles of birth, death, and renewal, and so forth. Under the governance of God, the cosmos works in a fashion comparable to a well-ordered community. The heavenly bodies and men alike "serve" their creator by bending themselves to his purposes and by rejoicing in his goodness to them.

Byrhtferth's *Manual,* an early eleventh-century compendium of chronological and cosmological data, underscores one aspect of the cosmic community. The rotations of the sun and planets are related to the earthly cycle of the seasons. But the annual cycles are also analogous to the course of human life. Spring (and one must remember that the year was as often regarded as beginning at Easter as in January, the first month of the Roman calendar) is like boyhood: both are moist and hot, as is blood, the predominant humor of boyhood, and air the predominant element of spring. Likewise summer, which is hot and dry, corresponds to early manhood. The related element and humor are fire and red bile. Autumn, dry and cold, corresponds to manhood, and its element, earth, with the humor of manhood, melancholy (black bile). Winter and manhood with their respective element and humor, water and phlegm, are likewise associated. Thus man's life cycle is related in the cosmic community to the rotations of spheres about the earth in accordance with natural law.

In a sense, then, man is a minute world or balancing of natural forces, a microcosm which can best be understood in comparison with the macrocosm. One aspect of this relationship is alluded to in a familiar poetic motif (and one which is not at the moment very congenial to many young people). In *The Wanderer,* to cite one of several examples, it is stated that a man cannot be wise until he has experienced his proper portion of winters and that he should exercise patience until he attains understanding. One suspects that the poet thinks of early manhood as, like summer, a season of vigor but of unripeness and of autumn or harvest time, like manhood, as a precious moment of maturity, vigor, and wisdom. Although the author of *The Wanderer* has no occasion to dwell upon the subject, there is the sense in other Old English poems that man progresses from a spring seedling to a physically robust summer plant to a final wintry state in which wisdom, now harvested, remains intact but is bereft of strength. The complex reflections on age, strength, and wisdom in *Beowulf*, which pivot upon Hrothgar's sermon in lines 1700–1784, reflect this understanding of the life cycle. The emphasis on Beowulf's youth, maturity, and age and his relationships with his elders Hrothgar and Hygelac, seem to imply this notion of the life of man within the natural order.

The cosmos or created order was, in the accepted view, finite; it had a beginning and would end, and its existence could be delimited by six ages which were considered comparable with the six days of creation. Byrhtferth was but one of several writers who gave thumbnail sketches of universal history in these terms. The ages ran from Adam to Noah, from Noah to Abraham, from Abraham to David, from David to the Babylonian exile, from the exiles' return to Jerusalem to the birth of Christ, and, finally, from the coming of Christ to his second coming. The Last Judgment would, it was believed, inaugurate the eternal Sabbath rest, comparable to the rest of the creator on the seventh day. In part because of the much-stressed assertion of the Gospels that the Second Coming would be preceded by the reign of the Antichrist—the apotheosis of depravity and the nadir of history—and in part because of the adoption of the ancients' belief that the world itself was aging, it was frequently asserted that the world in its sixth age was in a stage of decay and declining strength. This fact accounted for the instability of both natural and political history. The world, like man, was growing old and feeble and, therefore, was deteriorating both in strength and dependability.

This last aspect of early medieval cosmology is but one of several manifestations of a general feeling at that time that man must expect to experience seemingly irrational and undeserved hardships. Fatalism has often—and rightly—seemed a prominent theme of Old English literature, and *wyrd* (fate) has become the best-known word in the Old English vocabulary. Often this fatalism has seemed to critics to be a direct inheritance from the Germanic world view. Against the irrationality of fate, man could only persevere. "Fate," remarks E. O. G. Turville-Petre, "will decide the moment and manner of your death, but fate will not decide how you will face it. A brave death will be rewarded, not with pork and mead as in Valhöll, but with the esteem of your friends, kinsmen, and even your enemies." The problem is a universal one; indeed, it is the problem Boethius sought to answer in a not dissimilar way in *The Consolation*.

Whatever the sources of Anglo-Saxon fatalism, one must always at least consider the possibility when he meets *wyrd* in the literature that it is to be understood in the general framework of cosmology in which Alfred defines it in his *Boethius*. In a passage of the same chapter which contains the wagon wheel parable, Alfred defines fate as an aspect of providence. It is God's daily adjustment of providence or foreknowledge actuated in the world. The wagon wheel passage serves primarily to clarify this point. What man sees as senseless fate is part of providence, controlling events in accordance with the dictates of a wisdom beyond human comprehension by reaching out to correct man's misuse of his freedom to do God's will. Man's good fortune or prosperity is not subject to fate, for prosperity is controlled by the forethought of God. Rather, "Wyrd is God's work of adjusting the world to embrace the contingencies that arise as men choose their particular course of action." Thus, ultimately, fate is a beneficent force, however irrational or cruel it may appear to be from the standpoint of the man who is subject to its operations.

Much more could be said about Anglo-Saxon cosmological beliefs, but for the present the reader who would like to know more must be referred to Bede and Byrhtferth. Students of literary backgrounds have sometimes been accused of overemphasizing these matters; and, in the case of the background of Old English literature, the danger of overemphasis is very real. The Anglo-Saxon writers accepted the world picture or cosmology of the late classical writers. Unlike Middle English writers, however, they did not dwell extensively on matters of cosmology or make carefully detailed applications of cosmological lore. Impatient and unprepared to deal with the logical niceties of the Neoplatonic cosmos, they tended rather to employ the world picture to underline their belief that the creation functioned under the moral governance of the creator, that man was free and had the responsibility to act in accordance with his dictates, and that God judges man with reference to his use of his freedom. Thus the orbiting spheres of Boethius became the wagon wheels of Alfred. Life was like the wheel in that the man who put himself next to the axle and made the right use of his freedom traveled with the least disturbance. And the world was like the wheel in that it was a morally mixed community of men at the center and on the periphery, who were mutually dependent upon each other and upon the creative support of God, the axle. Thus, while the cosmological picture was accepted, it lost its metaphysical implications and gained moral urgency.

B. The Ordering of Life in the World

To secure the order and moral governance of the world was the task of appointed rulers acting under the guidance and dictates of law, both civil and ecclesiastical. Fortunately, a great body of legal codes and other documents survives from the Anglo-Saxon period and provides the student with the surest guide to the structures of social and political life.

The following passage on kingship is extracted from the most extended and sophisticated Old English tract on law, Archbishop Wulfstan's *Institutes of Polity, Civil and Ecclesiastical.* As a late document, both in the history of Anglo-Saxon law and in the career of the great bishop and legislator, it represents the culmination of legal development and provides a convenient summary and background for a consideration of the social organization of the Anglo-Saxons.

Concerning the King:

It is very rightly fitting for the Christian king that he should stand in the place of a father to the Christian people and be the regent of Christ, as he is considered, with respect to care and protection. It is also proper that he should love Christianity with all his power and detest heathendom and that he should always eagerly honor and defend God's church and give peace and reconciliation to all Christian people with more equitable law, as he can most zealously do. And by this means he shall become great in God, if he love right and shun wrong.

Concerning the Kingdom:

There are eight columns which firmly uphold the righteous kingdom: truth and patience and liberality and reasonableness and fear of evil and furtherance of the good and lightness of taxation and justice. And seven things befit the just king: the first, that he have great fear of God; and second that he ever love justice; and third, that he be gentle towards the good. And fourth, that he be stern towards the sinful. And fifth, that he always help the needy. And sixth, that he further and protect God's church. And seventh, that he guide with proper judgment friend and stranger alike.

Every throne which stands perfectly aright rests on three supports: the first is *Oratores*, the second *Laboratores*, the third is *Bellatores*. *Oratores* are priests, who must serve God and pray eagerly both day and night in behalf of the entire nation. *Laboratores* are workers, who have to provide that by which the entire population is able to live. *Bellatores* are warriors, who must defend the country in a warlike way with their weapons. On these three supports every throne ought to stand with justice. And should any of them weaken, the throne immediately will totter; and if any of them break, then the throne will fall down; and that damages the whole nation. But if one makes them steadfast, and strengthens and fortifies them eagerly by means of God's true law, that will be to the lasting benefit of the people.

Thus what I say is true: if Christianity weaken, the kingdom immediately totters. And if one disseminate unlawfulness or vice anywhere in the land too widely, that will damage the entire nation. But if one does what he ought, if he abandons injustice and takes up God's justice, that can be a benefit in the sight of God and the world. Amen.

The *Institutes of Polity* is a compendium of general reflections upon both secular and ecclesiastical law, based on the best available commentaries by Christian students of the law. Its organization and diction and the evidence of continuous revision by the author show that Wulfstan was making an effort to assemble a tract which would, according to Professor Bethurum, crown "his life-long effort to bring order into a disordered society." The passage quoted above draws on Sedulius Scotus, a ninth-century Irish poet and theologian who worked on the Continent under Carolingian patronage, on Ælfric of Eynsham, who frequently supplied the Archbishop with homiletic and legal data, and on several collections of canon law. In later versions, the passage was considerably revised and amplified in the direction of greater clarity and comprehensiveness. Perhaps the most interesting alteration for our present purposes was the addition of several introductory sentences on the kingship of God which render the comments on the earthly king as father of his people and regent of Christ less striking but more traditional.

Archbishop Wulfstan was an extremely important transitional figure in the history of English law. Recent stylistic and historical studies have identified him as the author of much of the significant legislation of the early eleventh century. Ecclesiastical influence on the development of secular law was by no means without precedent in the Old English period, but the work of Wulfstan took place against the background of the monastic revival of the preceding century which had fostered an atmosphere of cooperation between the king and the chief ministers of the church, and it represents the apogee of this relationship in England. In the century after Wulfstan, the new codifiers of ecclesiastical law (who were important contributors to the "intellectual revolution" mentioned in Chapter I) were to foster a sense of opposition between secular and canon law which radically transformed the political atmosphere of Europe in general and of England in particular. In the first quarter of the eleventh century, however, Wulfstan's notion of the king as standing "in the place of a father to the Christian people" and as "regent of Christ" represented both the ideal and actual practice.

The legislative relationship of church and king can be traced in England to the earliest written code of the Anglo-Saxons, the Laws of Æthelberht of Kent (c. 602), but the exact nature of the partnership and certain features of later development can be understood only in the light of several much earlier traditions.

Both in England and on the Continent, certain peculiar characteristics seem to differentiate the Germanic from the Roman legal tradition. The most striking difference is that, whereas Roman law was based upon legislated codes, Germanic law was customary. That is to say, the law consisted not of written prescriptions or codes but of traditions passed orally from generation to generation. Tribal leaders seem to have been regarded as the custodians of the law. They were not legislators in the sense that they made laws; rather they decided in a given instance what the law and the prescribed penalty were. As the Germans settled in areas which had been part of the Roman Empire, they usually applied the principle, called "the personality of the law," that a given man was subject—no matter where he lived—to the legal customs of his own people. Thus, at least in the beginning, the tradition of Roman law was maintained for the old inhabitants of the Empire. In time, however, law tended to become territorial, as ethnic distinctions among inhabitants of an area broke down. The extent to which the personal, as opposed to the territorial, concept of law was maintained depended in large part upon geographical factors: the more deeply Romanized an area, the more likely it was that territoriality would come to prevail. Under the influence of Roman tradition, written codifications of Germanic law came to be made. The famous Frankish codes (Salian and Ripuarian) are fruits of this process and are regarded as among the best sources for relatively pure Germanic traditions.

Because of the breakdown of Roman administration, the legal customs of the Anglo-Saxons who settled in Britain were probably relatively free from the influence of Roman law before the coming of the missionaries in the last decade of the sixth century. It is also generally believed that the civic organization of Anglo-Saxon England maintained Germanic institutions in a comparatively pure form except for the modifications necessary to accommodate the new religion. Of this confrontation and amalgamation of Germanic customary and Roman codified law, the short code of Æthelberht of Kent is the first evidence, although the only copy is in the twelfth-century manuscript collection known as *Textus Roffensis*. Bede refers to the code and remarks on its importance:

> Among the many benefits that [Æthelberht's] wisdom conferred on the nation, he introduced, with the consent of his counsellors, a code of law framed on the Roman pattern, which was written in English, and remains in force to this day. The first of his laws is designed to protect the Church he embraced, and decrees that satisfaction must be made by any person who steals property from the Church, the bishop, or other clergy.
>
> (*Ecclesiastical History* II. 5)

Bede's comments are both misleading and instructive. Clearly he recognized the novelty of Æthelberht's written code: it was "framed on the Roman pattern." It was nevertheless clearly a codification of Germanic custom, not legislated by the king but simply recorded with the consent of councillors. Its Romanism lies not in its content but in the mere fact that it was reduced to writing. But the importance of this "mere fact" would be difficult to overestimate. The occasion for writing the document was the conversion of the king, which resulted in the adoption of a new institution which had its own laws and traditions and to which no analogous institution had ever existed in Kent. It was, therefore, necessary to define the relationship of the church to the existing society by making room for it within the body of formerly oral custom. The reader of the code soon realizes, however, that it is more concerned to state the secular customs than to define the role of Christian institutions, as he might reasonably have inferred from Bede's description. Thus the original purpose of the code may have been to provide the ecclesiastics with a memorandum outlining the chief aspects of Kentish customary law. The accommodation of the customs to the presence of the new priestly class appears to be a secondary purpose of the document, although the coming of the missionaries was clearly the occasion for recording the customary law. The fact, duly noted by Bede, that the laws of Æthelberht were written in Old English distinguishes them from the Continental Germanic codes, all of which were recorded in Latin.

A brief account of the contents of the "laws of Æthelberht" can serve as an introduction to Anglo-Saxon law and social organization before we turn to an account of the period with which this book is primarily concerned. The first chapter of the code is the only one which deals with the church: it sets the amounts of compensation due for damage to the property of the church and of ecclesiastics and for breaches of the peace of the church. In comparison with the rates of compensation due the king and lesser laymen, it reveals that Æthelberht was prepared to accord the church an unusually high status. The chapter confines itself to issues between laymen and ecclesiastics, and the silence of the code with reference to other aspects of ecclesiastical life may indicate that the principle of personality of the law was silently accepted. The next group of chapters deals with compensations due the king; those due a nobleman (*eorl*) and a freeman (*ceorl*) follow. The next chapters discuss various kinds of legal compensations, notably the *wergild* or payment due the family of a man who has been wrongfully killed. A long series of laws deals with compensations for bodily injuries of every sort, and the last section of the code treats of injuries to women and the crimes of servants or slaves. Clearly the entire body of Kentish tradition has not been recorded. For example, allusion to the "protection" *(mundbyrd)* of king, eorl, and ceorl, to wergild, and to the liability of the family of a criminal should he leave the country imply the existence and importance of family law. Furthermore, beyond an allusion to occasions when "the king calls his people to him," nothing is said about the administration of the law. The society clearly has three chief classes: the king, the noblemen or eorls, and freemen or ceorls. Women have legal rights distinct from those of men, and servants are treated as property, the value of which depends to some extent upon the rank of the owner.

It has already been stated that the king was not regarded as the legislator but as the custodian of the law. As the custom of promulgating codes of law became established, this view (which implied that the customary law was all-inclusive) may have been eroded. At any rate, at the beginning of the period under consideration here, Alfred stated in the introduction to his laws that he had "collected" the laws "which I liked" after consultation with councillors. But even Alfred felt constrained to avoid too many innovations, "because it was unknown to me what would please those who should come after us." Thus his laws remained primarily a collection based on the written compilations of customary law from Æthelberht onwards. The concluding statement of Alfred's introduction is that his councillors consented to observe the finished code. This statement underlines the aspect of assent to the law which was stressed by Bede in his description of Æthelberht's code; the councillors recognized the written laws as an acceptable version of customary tradition.

There is also some evidence for the continued application of the concept of the personality of the law in the later period. "The Treaty between Alfred and Guthrum," for example, deals with legal issues which might arise between Alfred's people and the Danish settlers in the late 880s. It implies that each people would be governed internally by its own customs. That such a system actually existed is proved by the frequent use in the tenth and eleventh centuries of the term "Danelaw" to designate both the customs of the Danish settlers and the areas of England which they dominated. Actually, however, within the Danelaw territoriality prevailed: the English were granted equal status with the Danes, whose law was followed; and Danish supremacy did not, in fact, long persist. By the time of Wulfstan, "Danelaw" had come to refer to "the prevalence of Danish custom within a particular district." After the Conquest, it appeared for a time that a dual Saxon-Norman legal system would come into being; but the concept of territorial law won out, and the Normans in general adopted the English law, which was in most respects more sophisticated than their own.

With these factors as elements of the historical background of Wulfstan's legal thought, it is now possible to consider one of the several eleventh-century legal documents to which he contributed. The "Laws of Cnut" were published in the early 1020s for the great Danish king of England and continued to be studied widely after the Conquest. Although the code is a late one, it is the culmination and crown of Anglo-Saxon legal history, and it demonstrates that Anglo-Saxon institutions had a remarkable continuity. As Sir Frank Stenton has said, "The men of Cnut's own time valued the code as a restatement of the good customs of the past by a king who was strong enough to enforce them."

The code has two divisions, ecclesiastical and secular, both of which have prologues declaring that they were promulgated by Cnut with his councillors from Winchester at their Christmas assembly in an unspecified year. The ecclesiastical code recapitulates laws of earlier kings and conflates these prescriptions with homiletic material, much of which is recognizably from the hand of Wulfstan. The first group of laws (I. 2–3) deals with sanctuary (*ciricgriδ*). The man who seeks sanctuary is comparable to a man who avails himself of the protection or peace of the king; and penalties, which vary according to the nature of the crime and the importance of the church in question, are set out for such offenses as murder, fighting, robbery, and sexual intercourse—all of which break the peace of Christ. The second group of ecclesiastical laws (4–5) treats of the manner in which the clergy are to clear themselves of accusations of crime. They must, sometimes with fellow clerics as supporters, prove themselves guilt-less by saying Mass. This means of clearing oneself was compa-rable to the secular ordeal, which will be discussed below. The clergy are divided into classes: seculars are distinguished from monks and, whether secular or regular, priests are distinguished from deacons. Later sections of the ecclesiastical code deal with the deportment of clerics, church dues, and festivals of the church calendar. Among the homiletic passages of the code, the most interesting exhort men to be loyal to their lords and lords to be faithful to their retainers because God expects such loyalty among men (20). As the secular code is expounded, it should become clear to the reader that these regulations concerning the clergy and the life of Christians in general were adapted over the cen-turies to the general framework of social life which was set forth in the ancient customary law.

The secular code of Cnut is by far the longer part of the docu-ment. It opens with general statements concerning the theological sanctions for law and government (II. 1–2) and proceeds straight-way to injunctions against the sale of criminals as slaves to for-eigners, especially heathen, and too frequent use of the death penalty (3–4). Heathenism is proscribed (5); criminals are urged to repent (6–7); and coinage problems are discussed (8). Allusion is made to the regularization of weights and measures (9) and to the citizens' obligations to repair towns and bridges and do military service in times of need (10). (These latter obligations are called the *trimoda necessitas* by legal historians.) The follow-ing chapter (11) contains admonitions to act lawfully and love justice "before God and the world." These clauses are (like most of the code) drawn from earlier sets of laws, and in two manu-scripts retain the concluding "Amen" which was appropriate to their earlier setting. The next section (12–15) deals with the king's legal rights over his subjects, which include such cases as breach of royal protection, avoidance of military service, and the cases of fugitives and outlaws; it clarifies differences in custom between Wessex and Mercia and the Danelaw. Those guilty of false accusation are to have their tongues removed unless they redeem themselves by payment of their wergild (16). Except in cases reserved to the king, one is to seek justice in the local courts of the hundred or the borough or at the higher shire-court (17–18); if one cannot obtain justice locally, he may appeal (19). Every free man over the age of twelve must be part of a hundred if he is to have a claim to his legal rights and is to be under surety that he will abide by the law and seek justice in the courts rather than by taking matters into his own hands (20–21).

The next group of laws (22–26) treats procedure in legal cases. In some cases, a man may clear himself of an accusation by a simple oath; in others, he must be joined by a specified number of persons who swear with and for him; in still other cases, the accused must go to the ordeal to establish his innocence. The method of expurgation depends to a great extent upon the reputation of the accused. If, for example, he has a bad name in the hundred and three men join in an oath of accusation, he must go straight to the threefold ordeal (30). As other sources tell us, the first ordeal was that of cold water: the accused who floated when thrown into cold water was taken to be guilty. The second and third, both of which were performed in the church, involved carrying a red-hot iron or taking a stone from a pot of boiling water. Innocence was established if the wounds healed in three days. One of the persistent problems faced by the Anglo-Saxon legislators was assuring that men would be available to the courts when they were accused. The requirement of surety was aimed at remedying this fault, and laws requiring the lord to stand surety for his retainer (30.1, 30.6, 31) are directed to the same end. The requirement that a friendless man or foreigner be imprisoned for want of surety until his trial (35) meets another aspect of the same problem. The strict laws (36–37) against taking false oaths—one might forfeit his lands or half his wergild to the lord and the bishop—combat a comparable difficulty inherent in a legal procedure which adjudicates according to the strength of oaths rather than the persuasiveness of factual evidence.

The following group of edicts establishes a hierarchy of legal values. Crimes committed during holy seasons or in holy places are especially heinous (38); and the higher the civil or ecclesiastical rank of the person offended, the greater the compensation required (38.1). The slaying of a cleric makes the killer an outlaw who must atone by exile and payment of wergild (39).

Since monks abandon the ties of kinship and can neither receive wergild for their kin nor have kin who would receive wergild on their deaths, the king is the recipient of their death-payments as well as those of foreigners who have no local protectors or kinsmen (40). Clergymen guilty of crime forfeit their orders and must go on penitential pilgrimages (41). The obligations of laymen are for the most part assumed in this section of the code.

After a series of chapters (45–57) designed to safeguard the church's seasons of feasting and fasting, there is a long list of laws (48–66) setting the compensations for a number of offenses which range from failure to pay church dues (fines which differ in the Danelaw and English law), adultery (the penalties vary according to the status of the woman—married, unmarried, nun, widow), and concubinage (excommunication) to treason against king or lord (death and forfeiture of property) and breach of peace while on military service (forfeiture of life and wergild). There follow two chapters (67–68) which stress the importance of correcting wrongdoers and bringing them back into the fold. Because the weak can bear less, one must "distinguish reasonably between age and youth, wealth and poverty, freedom and slavery, health and sickness" whether he is administering civil justice or ecclesiastical penance (68.1b–1c). To this end, the reeves are instructed to supply provisions for the king from the royal property and not by taxation of the people (69). Similar provisos protect the heirs of those who die without leaving a will. Their lords are forbidden to exact more than the legal heriot— the war-equipment with which the lord invested his men and which, unless the man died in battle in the lord's behalf (78), was to be returned at death—and required to direct the just distribution of the remainder of the property between the widow and other kinsmen (70). To avoid ambiguity, the laws designate the amounts of the heriots of earls and thegns, the latter being distinguished as to their closeness to the king (72), again taking account of differences in custom in various areas of England. Some attention is given to the estates of "householders" (73); and widows, who are forbidden to marry again within a year of the death of their husbands, are treated with an eye both to the fulfillment of their legal obligations and to the protection of their rights to property and to free choice in the matter of remarriage (74).

The final chapters are miscellaneous. One deals with the manner in which an innocent man whose weapons have been used by others in acts of violence may clear himself (75). Another states that, when a man brings stolen property into his cottage, his wife (unless she has locked the goods in her storeroom) and children do not share his guilt (76). Desertion of one's lord, hunting rights and the like are also touched upon (77–83). The homiletic conclusion (84) urges all men to love God and his law.

The Laws of Cnut are an impressive code. Profoundly traditional and marked by an equally impressive and sincere Christian understanding of the nature of kingship and of law, they reach an admirable balance between severity and compassion. It is clear that the code takes for granted many details of the legal system—that it is not, so to speak, a constitution. Yet it also leaves the impression of being by intent and in effect a comprehensive compilation of the most important aspects of royal law. The term "compilation" is important if one is to appreciate the traditionalism of the efforts of Cnut and Wulfstan here. The code frequently adopts the phraseology of earlier laws, especially those of Edgar and Æthelweard; and, even where the sources are unknown, there is probably no intention to be innovative. The laws are the fruit of years of compiling civil and ecclesiastical law and represent a distillation of the results of those labors. They reflect in the realm of law the general tendency in the Early Middle Ages to collect and preserve what is traditional and authoritative. In this respect, as in others, the Laws of Cnut bring to culmination the history of early medieval English law and anticipate the great legal studies of the following century which imposed rational order upon the confusing array of compilations of canon and secular law from the Early Middle Ages.

Even the casual student has not far to look for connections between these laws which Wulfstan did so much to shape and the Archbishop's *Institutes of Polity*. Not only do phrases from the one occasionally appear in the other, but the Laws are informed by the same high doctrine of Christian kingship which is embodied in the *Institutes*. Perhaps more important, however, is the fact that the Laws demonstrate one thing obscured by the generally Latinate and ecclesiastical tone and content of the *Institutes:* that, however they were changed by the introduction of the church as an institution and by the very concept of written law, the Anglo-Saxon legal traditions and social institutions have a strong continuity of their own which is tacitly assumed by the episcopal legislator.

As the code itself implies, the society for which the Laws of Cnut were written was comprised basically of three classes of men. At the summit was the king who stood alone, although he had his chief administrative officers, the *ealdormen* or earls, who had oversight of regions of the country (shires). Men of the second or upper class were called at various times *eorls* or companions *(gesithas)* or *thegns*. The third class were the freemen, commonly referred to as *ceorls*. Slaves were treated by the laws more as chattels than as persons, although the church throughout the period encouraged manumission, which usually raised them to the status of ceorls. The distinctions among these classes were made with regard to the property they owned and the amounts of their wergilds. Both varied from time to time and place to place. The sum which the law required be paid the kinsmen of a slain man by his killer, however, was typically two hundred shillings for a ceorl and twelve hundred for a thegn. It is difficult to work out equivalents with modern values, but the sums were considerable. The West-Saxon ceorl's wergild in the tenth century was, for example, the equivalent of the price of thirty-three oxen or two hundred sheep.

The nobility or thegns often had extensive estates. The minimal requirements, according to one eleventh-century document, were an estate of at least five hides of land, a function of some honor and a seat in the king's hall, and (on his own estate) a church, kitchen, bellhouse, and gate *(i.e.,* fortification). The thegn's land was usually "bookland," which is to say that it was exempt from the usual royal taxes except for the universal obligations of military service and the repair of bridges and fortresses. The ceorl was any free man not recognized as a thegn. Some of these were landholders but, especially in the tenth and eleventh centuries when the economic status of ceorls as a class had declined, many were tenants and dependants of the nobility.

Women, especially those of the noble class concerning whom the evidence is more abundant, had considerable freedom under Anglo-Saxon law, especially when their status is compared with that under feudal law after the Conquest. They could own, inherit, and dispose of property; and they could appear before the courts in their own behalf. Allusion has already been made to chapters 73–74 of II Cnut which safeguarded the legal rights of widows and the rights of all women to freedom of decision as to whether or not to marry. Another legal fragment treats of property and other rights which are to be considered when a betrothal is contracted. If, for example, the bride is to move to the jurisdiction of a thegn other than the one under whom she formerly lived, "it is to her interest that her friends have the assurance that no wrong will be done to her" and that she will be treated fairly in court.

There were several kinds of courts by the tenth century, as the Laws of Cnut imply. Areas called hundreds (or in the Danelaw *wapentakes)* held court or *folk-moot* monthly. The shire court met every six months. The king's reeve presided over the former; the bishop and ealdorman or earl had oversight of the shire-moot, at which, in addition to adjudication of cases, royal writs were promulgated. The nobility often had the right to administer justice on their estates, but there is little concrete evidence concerning the administration of private law. Above all, of course, was the king's court, which did not so often administer law as state what was the law. The fact that royal codes customarily mention the assent of councillors to the royal definitions of law shows that codes were promulgated at meetings of the council or *witenagemot.*

Discussion of one prominent factor in Anglo-Saxon law has been reserved for the end to stress its importance. This is the bonds of loyalty, which were the very cement of Anglo-Saxon society. Several chapters of II Cnut may be taken as typical:

57. And if anyone plots against the king or his lord, he is to forfeit his life and all that he owns, unless he goes to the threefold ordeal. . . .

77. And the man, who in his cowardice deserts his lord or his comrades [*geferan*], whether it is on an expedition by sea or on land, is to forfeit all that he owns and his own life; and the lord is to succeed to the possessions and to the land which he previously gave him. . . .

78. And the heriot is to be remitted for the man who falls before his lord in a campaign, whether it is within the land or outside the land. . . .

Along with such provisions, one should keep in mind the reverence of the codes for the ties of kinship—symbolized by the continuing strength of the customs concerning wergild—and its concern for the "friendless" man. Loyalties, expressed legally in terms of mutual obligations, to one's kinsman or to his "protector" or lord, require one's wholehearted acceptance. Their breach invokes the society's most severe punishments. The bonds of kinship gave rise to the duty of seeking revenge and thus to the blood-feud which sometimes threatened the peace of society at large and came under increasingly severe regulation, often at the insistence of churchmen. The retention of the wergild and the increasing use of fines as compensation for crimes tended to mitigate the more barbarous consequences of the customs of kinship and blood-feud. The obligations of clients to their lords, however, continued to be revered and to be reinforced by the laws, whether with reference to the upper or military classes or to the tenants of the landed. The relationships can, not unjustly, be compared with those of kinship, for they are the creations of tradition which bring artificial familial ties into being.

This last observation brings us back to Wulfstan's *Institutes of Polity*. The last and most ambitious Anglo-Saxon theoretical legal treatise is framed by just such an observation. In Wulfstan's original draft, he specifically states that the king stands as a father to his people. The bonds of loyalty, of artificial but nonetheless vital kinship, bind king and subject. If the Archbishop abandoned the image of fatherhood in later versions, he nevertheless retained what must have seemed to him an analogous idea by speaking of God as the "best of all kings" and of the earthly king as his vicar. The expression has become a bit less striking and more cautious, but it is doubtful that Wulfstan believed he had altered his basic position. Certainly as he proceeded, he continued to stress in his metaphoric references to the columns or supports of the body politic the interrelatedness and interdependence of the segments of society and the necessity of concern for the well-being of the whole.

Wulfstan holds an important place in legal history and commands respect and admiration. If the law of his tradition is hierarchical and undemocratic, these characteristics are not unexpected. If it is sometimes harsh in its punishments and reflects situations which seem primitive and even barbaric, it is also always concerned to distribute justice more fairly and temperately and to mitigate the basic evils of the society. Above all, it is concerned to create for men—and women—not only a sense but also a condition of relatedness by means of personal loyalties; or, in the hateful jargon of our times, "meaningful relationships." One can think of many legal systems, both much earlier and much later, which were more repressive and less concerned to understand and to effect justice.

C. Loyalties in the World

Then those who did not want to be there retreated from the battle. Odda's sons were the first to flee there: Godric went from the battle and abandoned the good man [Byrhtnoth] who had often given him many a horse; he leapt upon the steed which belonged to his lord, onto the saddle—which was not lawful—; and both his brothers, Godwine and Godwig, galloped with him. They cared not for war but turned from the battle and sought the forest, fled into the fastness and saved their lives. And more men fled than was at all proper if they had remembered all of the favors which [Byrhtnoth] had done for their benefit. It was as Offa told him on a previous day when he held a moot in the meeting place: that many men spoke boldly there who afterwards, in a moment of need, would not hold out.

(lines 185–201)

The Battle of Maldon commemorates a battle against a Viking band in the year 991 in which Byrhtnoth, the ealdorman of Essex, lost his life. One hesitates in the light of recent discussions of the poem to approach it as an historical document, for it has been shown that it can hardly be regarded as a journalistic report of the battle. Let it be clear at the outset, then, that the poem is not being studied for the historical facts it may reveal but for the attitude of the author toward his subjects. More specifically, our topic is the poet's assumptions regarding the nature of heroism, or loyalty to a secular lord.

The passage selected for special attention describes the flight of three brothers after the death of the ealdorman. Later in the poem (lines 237b–243) one Offa, who seems to have been second in command under Byrhtnoth, speaks of the consequences of

Godric's flight upon the leader's horse: others in the formation, not knowing Byrhtnoth was dead, had thought the ealdorman himself was retreating when they saw his mount being ridden away and had broken ranks, seriously worsening the situation for loyal members of the band of fighters from Essex. Thus the flight of the sons of Odda is a strong negation of the ideal of loyalty to one's lord: the three brothers represent exactly what one is supposed *not* to do.

II Cnut 77, which prescribes forfeiture of life and property for desertion of one's lord during a military expedition, seems to cover cases just such as those of Godric, Godwine, and Godwig. Chapter 78 of the same code, which releases the lands of those who die in battle with their lord from the obligation of heriot, deals with the reverse situation. But the suggested date for the Laws of Cnut is 1020–23, and the chapter is from a section of the code for which there are no clear extant sources. A code of Æthelred, which is dated 1008, covers only cases of desertion arising when the king himself is leading the army. Thus there is no contemporary testimony to the legal consequences of the desertion of the brothers in *The Battle of Maldon*. Perhaps the obligations of loyalty to one's lord in battle—the obligations in which Godric and his brothers were deficient—had been axiomatic in the earlier period. They may have been taken for granted in customary law and, thus, not have been stated explicitly in the codes. At least in the eyes of the *Maldon* poet, there is no reason to believe that the traditional obligation of loyalty was seriously undermined in the late tenth century. If the poet expressed an opinion shared widely by his contemporaries and if the situation had caused widespread difficulties in this period of renewed Viking attack, the strong provisions of II Cnut may make the customs of loyalty explicit in an effort to revive and revitalize them. At least a possibility exists that the tradition of loyalty had become impractical or anachronistic or both.

The historical context in which the poem is set suggests that in fact the stage was not one on which the traditions of loyalty, commonly called the ideal of the *comitatus,* were likely to be acted out in an ideal fashion. Æthelred II came to the throne in 978, succeeding his half-brother Edward. The circumstances

surrounding the death of Edward indicate that members of Æthelred's household were responsible, though probably without the
young prince's complicity; and that Edward soon came to be
regarded as a martyr and was the focus of a considerable cultus
are only among the evidences of the suspicion which many subjects entertained of the new king. Æthelred, who reigned until
1016, was ineffectual as a soldier and seems to have been plagued
by persistent suspicions of his motives. The situation is symbolized
by the epithet which is still commonly attached to his name:
Unræd, "No-Counsel." This is not the place to sketch the details
of that unhappy reign, but there is one aspect—Æthelred's re-
lations with the Vikings—which demands mention. English political confusion and new Scandinavian unity under Danish leadership led to the revival of large-scale raids. Shortly after the
battle of Maldon (but not entirely as a consequence of that
battle), Æthelred, on the advice of the Archbishop of Canterbury,
entered into a treaty with the Danes, paying "twenty-two thousand pounds of gold and silver" for the truce, to little avail. The
ultimate outcome, indeed, was the accession of Cnut upon the
death of Æthelred's heir, Edmund, just seven months after the
death of his father.

A number of *Chronicle* entries suggest a general failure of
nerve among the subjects of Æthelred. In 993, Ealdorman Ælfric
warned the Danes of an impending English attack and then de-
serted his own army. The following year, three leaders of the
English army fled the battlefield. Archbishop Wulfstan's fulminations in the famous *Sermo Lupi ad Anglos* described the moral
decay of his countrymen most vividly: loyalty is on the decline;
kinship is disregarded; slaves rise against masters; the clergy are
slack in the performance of their duties. "The weakening of the
sense of loyalty and personal duty towards the king, shown in
the conduct of many persons . . . ," Stenton concludes, "seems to
have been accompanied by a general disregard of social obligations." And not a few contemporary observers recognized and
deplored the situation. Against this background, one is tempted
to argue that Godric and his brothers are more typical representatives of English society than those who chose to die on the
field where their lord had fallen. The poet, who depicts the flight

of the sons of Odda immediately after the death of Byrhtnoth, makes these two events the pivot of his narrative.

Another, related aspect of the poem needs to be stressed. Unusual emphasis is placed upon the loyalty of Byrhtnoth the Ealdorman to Æthelred his king. It may well be wrong to urge too insistently that the poet consciously plays the disloyalty of the cowards against the loyalty of Byrhtnoth. But the contrast is there, and it becomes the more striking in the light of the historical background. Æthelred is mentioned three times in *The Battle of Maldon*. First, during the *flyting* or exchange of taunts which precedes the battle, Byrhtnoth instructs the Viking messenger to tell his people "that there stands here an undaunted earl with his / band who intends to defend his homeland—the country / of my lord Æthelred—the people and the ground" (lines 51–54a). Again, during the battle, Byrhtnoth is referred to as "the noble thegn of Æthelred" (line 151); and immediately after the description of the flight of the sons of Odda, there is a sentence which restates the fact of Byrhtnoth's death, calling him "lord of the people, Æthelred's earl" (lines 202b–203a). Any of these instances alone would be slight. But taken together, especially in the light of the first reference to Æthelred as lord of the land, they amount to a fairly emphatic statement of the loyalty of the ealdorman to his king. He is always conscious of his station and his obligations, as are only some of his retainers; and the sophistication of the poet's understanding of kingship may be compared favorably with that of Wulfstan in the *Institutes of Polity*.

Finally, of course, there are ringingly positive statements of the ideal of loyalty in *The Battle of Maldon*. Of these the most famous is probably that of Bryhtwold, the "old retainer," in lines 312–319. The rhetorical balance and grandeur of its opening statement that qualities of mind and heart must wax as physical strength wanes has invariably moved students of the poem. There follows a comment on the life of perpetual lamentation to which the deserters have consigned themselves; and finally the old man —and age is often, as here, equivalent to wisdom—states his resolve not to leave the battlefield alive but to lie beside his dead lord.

Another side to heroism is expressed in several statements in the poem. It is put best by Byrhtnoth himself in the conclusion of the speech in which *for his ofermode* ("because of his pride," line 89b) he allows the Vikings to cross the bridge so that they can be engaged in combat: "God alone knows who will be able to control the field of battle" (lines 94b–95). One almost expects the word *wyrd* to appear here and again in the rather laconic statement of lines 104b–105 that the time had come for men who were doomed to die *(fæge men)*. In his dying prayer (lines 173–180) Byrhtnoth commends himself to God's protection and thanks God for the joys of his life with no sign of impatience or despair. In these comments, one has a statement of resignation in the face of "what happens" to a man, a theme discussed theoretically by Alfred in the adaptation of Boethius and a commonplace as well of speeches before battle. Not only is the hero loyal to his ideals, to his code of conduct; he is also confident in the knowledge that, having lived by his code, he has done all that a man can do. "What happens" is not so important as how he has lived. Consolation is an aspect of heroism. It leads not so much to resignation as to confidence that one can do what he must. The obverse is failure of nerve, or attempt to manipulate "what happens." A *mæg gnornian* ("may he ever mourn," line 315) is not so much a curse on the cowards as a statement of the inevitable psychological consequences of cowardice.

Behind the treatment of the problem of loyalty in *The Battle of Maldon* there lie, in addition to the cultural expectation of standards of deportment, certain assumptions of fact concerning military organization; and these must be discussed briefly even at the risk of apparent lapse into unprofitable and fallacious search for verisimilitude in the verse. According to the most recent students of late Anglo-Saxon military institutions, the army had three divisions. The first was composed of mercenaries, usually few in number but the most expert soldiers. The other two divisions are referred to collectively as the *fyrd* or levy. The "select" fyrd was composed of freemen, normally thegns, but sometimes ceorls, who were levied representatives of land areas, usually five-hide units. This group served as much as two months a year when they were called for service, customarily by the king. Finally, there was the "general" fyrd composed of all freemen and usually summoned for purposes of local defense. At

Maldon, the force assembled seems to have consisted of mercenaries and the select fyrd. The former were Byrhtnoth's personal retainers (*heorðwerod,* line 24) among whom he stationed himself after he had marshalled the members of the select fyrd. The incomplete opening passage of the poem seems to indicate that many in Byrhtnoth's force at Maldon were unseasoned and cocky; and Offa seems also to have implied as much when he asserted (lines 198–201) that many of those who had made rash boasts before battle would suffer loss of courage when confronted with the realities of warfare. The raids of 991, indeed, were the beginning of the consistent series of Viking invasions which were to plague Æthelred for the rest of his reign; heretofore the raids had been intermittent. At least in part, the crisis of loyalty and courage at Maldon may be ascribed to the meeting of a fyrd, the members of which had not often (if ever) been summoned before, with an army of seasoned professionals. The shield-wall formation used by Byrhtnoth was a closely packed infantry formation in which the household troop of the ealdorman probably held the van and the members of the select levy were to the rear. The archers would have been even further behind. Thus the less-experienced were both safer and more out of touch with the course of events in the front of the battle line.

Thus far, it has been shown that *The Battle of Maldon* is a poem concerned with the theme of the obligations of loyalty in circumstances which were not conducive to the fulfillment of the ideal. At the same time, it is dressed both in the rhetoric and the conventions of the literary tradition of heroism. It prefaces the battle with flytings hurled between the opposing armies. Speeches evoke the highest heroic sentiments. The ravens and the eagle—though without their usual companion, the wolf—are ready for carrion (lines 106–107). If the attitude of Beowulf's cowardly retainers during the hero's last battle with the dragon can be taken as a likely element of other such tales, even the motif of faithlessness may be conventional. There is reference to the relationship of Byrhtnoth to his *swustersunu* ("sister's son," line 115), Wulfmær; and emphasis on the closeness of this relationship is not unusual in a military context. The sounds of battle are evoked. Byrhtnoth is called a "giver of rings" (line 290).

A chief problem of the poem, M. J. Swanton has argued, is that most of these conventional details are anachronistic. The details of heroic life do not fit the facts of life in the kingdom of Æthelred; and when one recognizes this fact, "the whole is seen to have been built upon false foundations, a travesty of antique heroic values." This argument has at least the merit of stressing anew the basic contrast of the poem between the real and the ideal: the failure of loyalty and the code of loyalty to which there was, at least formally, universal assent. It is true that the poet has hearkened to a genre of Old English poetry which no longer fit the case; and it is at least plausible that he was a gifted ironist, aware of the effect of the contrast. Yet *The Battle of Brunanburh,* which commemorates an event of 937 and cannot be much less anachronistic, avoids the dangers braved in *Maldon* by concentrating on panegyric of the hero and by avoiding too specific details.

Perhaps, given the similarities between the predicament of Godric and situations contemplated in some of the laws drafted by Archbishop Wulfstan, one could argue that the author of *The Battle of Maldon* had the same goal as the legislator: to reform and revitalize the nation by means of a revival of the traditional standards of loyalty. Professor Pope's view of the poem which is not inconsistent with this suggestion is that it is "a self-contained little tragedy, a revelation of men's strength under duress." The ealdorman in the first half of the poem as we have it shows himself a creditable representative of the ideal, despite circumstances which are not propitious. His death is followed hard by the defection of the cowards, an incident which forms a pivot and contrast for the depiction of the fortitude and loyalty of those who must almost surely die in the latter half of the piece. For most readers, in modern times at least, the poet has made his point successfully: there is far more to be gained by dying for the cultural ideals to which one gives assent than by saving his life at the cost of integrity and self-respect. But whatever the reader's conclusions, the poem chiefly testifies to the tenacity of the ancient idea of loyalty as the cement of society. It further testifies to the profound traditionalism of the Early Middle Ages.

D. The Exemplar of Loyalty and Heroism

Critics of Old English religious poetry have conventionally found that there is a "fusion or overlapping of secular heroic concepts and Christian tradition in a poetic style that is sometimes native Anglo-Saxon and sometimes borrowed from and fused with Latin rhetorical practices," to quote Professor Greenfield. Whether this judgment will—as I sincerely hope—continue to stand depends upon the future of the study of the Germanic ethos and of the character of early medieval Christianity. The latter field has been in the ascendency in recent years, and the result has been to narrow the range of ideas and images which can be treated as peculiarly Germanic or native at the same time that it has enhanced our appreciation of the unique qualities of the theological and intellectual atmosphere of the Early Middle Ages. A great deal remains to be done, and whatever is said about the mingling of sources must be put cautiously and tentatively.

But the best way to state the matter at this juncture is probably to assert that early medieval theology characteristically portrayed Christ as hero and judge. Heroism and justice were, as the two preceding chapters have tried to demonstrate, the most important aspects of leadership in general and kingship in particular. There is, in other words, a congruity between the approaches to the problems of salvation and of social order. Each reinforces the other and helps to explain it; and they are so inextricably related that to ask which came first is to reopen a fruitless debate. In what follows, then, an effort will be made to talk about two seminal theological notions and to show how they were related to commonly accepted social values without prejudging the questions of which is more ancient and which was dominantly influential. It is only indicative of the nature of the situation that these notions are actually described in terms of dramatic events: the descent into hell, in which Christ is depicted as hero-king, and the Last Judgment, in which he is judge-king.

One could turn to any number of Old English religious poems or prose homilies to demonstrate the points I want to make; and the selection of two passages from the often-neglected *Ascension* of Cynewulf is arbitrary.

1. *Christ as Hero and King.*

> Now has the holy one despoiled hell of all the tribute that it long ago unjustly swallowed into that place of strife. Now are the devils' warriors vanquished and in living torment abased and manacled, in hell's bottom stripped of power. The opposing terrors could not prosper in war, in the hurling of weapons, when the king of glory, protector of heaven's kingdom, did battle with his ancient foes by his unaided might, where he drew forth out of captivity from the enemies' stronghold the greatest of spoils, an untold multitude of folk, this same throng that you look on here. Soul's Savior and God's own Son, he will seek out now after war-play the gift-seat of heavenly spirits. Now that you know clearly who the lord is that leads this army, come forth boldly, joyful in heart, to meet your friends. Open the gates! The ruler of all will come in to you, the king, author of the works of old, into his city, with no small company. He will lead into the joy of joys the people whom he took from the devils by his singlehanded victory. Angels and men shall be at peace together henceforth for ever. There is a covenant between God and man, spiritually sancti-fied truth, love, life's hope, and all light's joy.

(lines 558–585)

The *Ascension* is based on sections of a homily of Gregory the Great for the feast of the Ascension; but in the passage quoted above, Cynewulf developed—apparently on suggestions in (or like those in) a Latin poem by Bede—a picture of Christ arriving at the gates of heaven, accompanied by those whom he had re-deemed from hell and a host of angels. The poet models the scene at the entry to heaven on Psalm 23 (Vulgate): someone within asks, "Who is this king of glory?" and a representative of the host of Christ replies that he is the ruler of heaven and earth.

The speaker describing Christ goes on to say that it is he who has harrowed hell of the "tribute" *(gafole,* line 559) it swal-lowed up long ago. He has defeated his opponent, as though in war, and released the captives in hell who now accompany him to the gates of heaven. Now, after his conflict, Christ is return-

ing to his own stronghold. The gates are to be opened for the
hero who has set up a new legal agreement or treaty (*wær*,
line 583) between God and man.

This same victory over Satan is mentioned later in the poem
when Cynewulf lists the seven "leaps" of Christ: his conception,
birth, crucifixion, descent from the cross, harrowing of hell, and
ascension (lines 713–743):

> The fifth leap was when he cast down the host of the inhabi-
> tants of hell into the pit of torment, bound the hostile king and
> spokesman of the adversaries with fiery fetters, where he lies yet
> in prison, made fast with chains and shackled with sins.

(lines 730–736a)

Thus the event of the harrowing is twice mentioned by Cynewulf
in connection with the ascension, and both times there is no
specific reference to the resurrection.

The origins of the doctrine of the descent into hell are dim.
Its biblical bases have usually been traced to such passages as
I Peter 3:19 and 4:6 which state that Christ preached to the
"spirits in prison." The motif seems originally to have been designed to extend the benefits of Christ's work to the Old Testament saints. Later, a second treatment of Christ's activity in
the interim between the crucifixion and the resurrection emerged:
a great act of Christ's to liberate the Old Testament saints. This
notion is the germ of the developed interpretation of the descent
into hell with the defeat of Satan and the release of his captives.
But the full development of the early medieval understanding of
the significance of the descent required the addition of a further
element. For many theologians and in the popular imagination,
the descent became not simply the occasion of the release of the
faithful patriarchs; it was the definitive act by which Christ
saved all men by breaking the power of Satan. As Caesarius of
Arles, a sixth-century preacher whose homilies were favorite
sources of the Anglo-Saxon homilists, put it, "He descended into
hell in order to rescue us from the jaws of the cruel dragon."
It was probably under the influence of just such reflections on
the motif that the phrase *descendit ad inferna* ("he descended
into hell") was added to the so-called Apostles' Creed. This
radical reinterpretation of the descent of Christ had an importance in theology in the eighth through the tenth centuries
which can hardly be overemphasized. It was particularly influen-

PLATE 2.
  The Harrowing of Hell (CHRISTUS INFERNUM DESPOLIAT).

∞ 139 ∞

tial in Old English literature. Leaving aside the numerous homiletic references, there are extended treatments in two poems, *The Descent into Hell* of the Exeter Book and *Christ and Satan* in the Junius manuscript. *The Dream of the Rood* ends with an allusion to the renewal of hope for those who had suffered in the fires of hell and to Christ's victorious expedition (*siðfate*, line 150). The motif was also popular among painters. One of a series of drawings collected at the beginning of a Psalter manuscript (Plate 2) depicts Christ as a figure of larger-than-human proportions who stands within a gateway holding a demon captive under his feet. He reaches down to pull numerous and eager men and women from the jaws of hell, depicted allegorically as a great dragon lying on its back with mouth agape. The caption reads, "Christ despoils hell."

A basic notion which lies behind the early medieval treatments of the descent (and the use of the Latin verb *despolio*, "rob," "plunder," in the picture caption) is that before the victory of Christ, men belonged by rights to Satan. Anselm of Canterbury, who was the great critic of the emphasis on the descent as the crucial moment of Christ's work for man's salvation, characterized the position of the proponents of the theory as asserting that man in Eden had "handed himself over to [Satan] freely" and was, therefore, legally obliged to serve Satan as his lord. The condition of Satan's thegns was, of course, indistinguishable from the most abject servitude. God in Christ came into the world in order to do battle with Satan and, by defeating him, to release mankind from his obligations of loyalty to the perverse lord; and for this heroic redemption, man became obliged to Christ as his lord.

The idea of loyalty, so basic an idea of Anglo-Saxon legal tradition, is in general accord with the understanding of the bonds of loyalty presupposed by the theological explanation of the descent of Christ into hell. The only difficulty is the fact that a transfer of loyalty from Satan to Christ is clearly allowed. But Satan's lordship was obtained by guile and, although his thegns were unable to free themselves from his lordship until a new champion appeared, they were free to enter into a covenant or treaty with the ransomer or redeemer because of the basic injustice of Satan's rule.

It is within this context that Cynewulf thinks of the matter in the lines quoted above. Hell is despoiled *(bireafod,* line 558) of its war-booty. Christ, unaided by others, did battle against all the forces hell had been able to muster. He won; and he released the throng which had been the greatest of Satan's spoils *(huþa mæste,* line 568). Now he returns to his proper kingdom with his new thegns, whom he has won in singlehanded victory *(þurh his sylfes sygor,* line 581). A new law or covenant or treaty is in force. The description of the fifth leap of Christ treats another aspect of the descent, the actual defeat of the evil king who wrongfully obtained man's allegiance: As a consequence, man becomes the subject of a new king and citizen of a different kingdom. The locus of salvation is the descent into hell because that is the event which makes possible the dissolution of one obligation of loyalty and the creation of another. Salvation is comprehensible only in the light of the most basic concept of social order.

2. *Christ as Judge and King.*

At the conclusion of the *Ascension,* Cynewulf incorporates his name in runic letters into a passage describing the Last Judgment. In the translation which follows, the modern equivalents of the runes are italicized.

> There many a man shall be led into the great assembly before the presence of the eternal Judge; when the *flame* trembles he shall hear the King speak, the Ruler of the skies utter stern words to those who formerly in the world were remiss in their obedience to Him, at a time when their *bow* and the *necessity* of the moment most easily availed to find help for them. There shall many a man in that place await, fearful and weary, what severe punishments He will decree according to deeds. *Joy* in earth's treasures is fled. *Manly strength,* his portion of life's delights, *wealth* on earth, had long been entombed by the *waterfloods.*

(lines 795–807a)

After his description of the "leaps" of Christ, Cynewulf speaks of the necessity for men to mount by leaps or good works to heaven *þær is hyht ond blis, / geþungen þegnweorud* ("where there is hope and joy, an excellent host of thegns," lines 750b–

751a). One should therefore live rightly, protected by angels from the devil's arrows. Judgment, he concludes is near: Christ who came once to earth will come again to judge. The passage quoted above is the beginning of a description of the Last Judgment.

Like the descent into hell the Doomsday scene plays a prominent role in Old English literature. There is an almost bewildering array of descriptions of the scene in the homiletic literature. Doomsday is also the setting of a number of poems, among which are *Christ III* (of which *Ascension* was once considered a part) in the Exeter Book, *Be Domes Dæge (Judgment Day I)* in an eleventh-century manuscript, and another Exeter poem called *Judgment Day II*. The topic is implicit at some point in almost every poem.

Although the Judgment scene is presented with a remarkable number of variations, its basic outline was established by the so-called Synoptic Apocalypse of Matthew, Mark, and Luke, the judgment parable of Matthew, 25:31–46, and the book of Revelation (Apocalypse). There might often be a discussion of the ages of the world and of the signs by which one was to perceive that the last hour was fast approaching. Among the signs were listed cosmic disasters, wars, and the rise of Antichrist—the incarnation of evil rulership. The world would be destroyed by fire, and at the sound of a trumpet all men would be raised from the dead to stand trial before Christ, who would assign men according to their merits to eternal punishment or to eternal joy with himself in his Kingdom of Heaven. There was not, comparatively speaking, very much speculation in the Early Middle Ages about the fate of the soul between man's death and the general resurrection, although some sort of continued existence was contemplated. Instead, the hopes of Christians were pinned primarily on the judgment scene, where Christ—like a king summoning his people to his court or assembly—would administer justice, banishing those who were disloyal and entering into a perfect fellowship with those who met his standards of loyalty. Given the emphasis on the bonds of loyalty in Anglo-Saxon social life and the lack of appreciation for metaphysical subtlety in the intellectual tradition, it becomes understandable that the problem of the destiny of the individual soul remained fairly undeveloped and that the picture of the great moot and judgment engaged far more attention. If Christ was the great hero who snatched men from the lord who had ensnared their loyalty, then the picture of ultimate salvation (of eschatology) was likely to be one which envisaged the creation of a perfectly loyal society under a perfect hero. And since the hero-king judges his retainers according to their loyalty or their fulfillment of the terms of the agreement under which they entered upon the relationship of lord and man, the biblical picture of the great assembly and judgment appealed to men as the definitive picture of what perfect life would be.

The dying Byrhtnoth in *The Battle of Maldon* prayed that angels would see him safely to God's protection (lines 175–180). The sentiment smacks of a doctrine of the soul which looks more to its immediate fate or immortality than to the Judgment. By far the more usual sort of prayer is that which Cynewulf wove into the conclusion of the *Ascension:* that men would pray for him so that he might be accepted at the Judgment as a thegn of Christ. He pictures the scene of the Judgment as a royal assembly *(gemot,* line 795), where the retainers must be frightened because they obeyed their lord so poorly. They relied on arms and the opportunities of the moment to give them apparent success, ignoring the standards which they knew had to prevail in the long run. All the things they had relied on will be gone at the Judgment: treasure, physical strength, and the like.

Cynewulf had two purposes in concluding his poem on the ascension with this passage. The more obvious, but less important, was to describe the ultimate outcome of Christ's ascension: the king who gained a new people by means of his heroism would judge his retainers by strict standards of loyalty. The second was, by weaving his name into the description, to commend himself to the prayers of his audience so that he himself might have a better chance of being judged mercifully. The device, unique in its use of runes but analogous to certain Latin name-acrostics, was an adaptation of rhetorical topics in which the writer modestly pleaded the inadequacy of his life and work and asked for the prayers of his audience.

In *Ascension*, then, one observes on several levels at one time the congruity of secular ideas of loyalty with the theological depiction of Christ. Christ is the hero who has won the loyalty and obedience of mankind and, consequently, he is the judge who must determine whether his retainers merit incorporation in his society. Society—whether in the world or in Christ's kingdom—is a matter of corporate relationships; and the individual defines, understands, identifies himself in terms of his obligations to a lord. Finally, one sees the individual, Cynewulf, asking for help to be found acceptable at the Lord's assembly.

E. Man as Alien

The Anglo-Saxons' reflections on the nature of life in this world emerge from and perhaps best integrate various elements in their backgrounds. Cynewulf's *Ascension* introduces the theme, which may be taken as a basic image of the human condition.

Cynewulf closes his poem with a simile (lines 850–865): a man's life in the world is like a ship; it is tossed by storms and tumults and struggles to get to a harbor where it can ride at anchor, in safety. The critics have been impressed by the expansion of what is merely a hint at the image in Cynewulf's source, Gregory's ascension sermon. Cynewulf employs what have been regarded as Germanic locutions; the ship, for example, is twice described with the kenning *sundhengest* ("seasteed," lines 852, 862). Actually, Gregory's allusion to the anchor of hope, which one must fix in the heavenly country, probably brought to the mind of the poet some such passage as the one from the preface to Gregory's *Dialogues* quoted above (page 68). In it the same comparison is made between secular life and the storm-tossed ship. For Gregory, the harbor had been the monastery, the life of contemplation; Cynewulf substitutes, for monasticism as the form of life best ordered to bring man to the goal of the Kingdom, the Kingdom itself. Life is hostile and uncertain, but one's voyage across the rough waters can lead to the harbor which Christ has offered. The theme of much of the greatest Old English poetry is precisely the same: this world is hostile to man, but the wise man understands that there is a realm at the end of the sea voyage in which he will not be an alien.

The great elegiac poem, *The Wanderer*, even more fully shows man as alien:

Thus I, often miserably sad, deprived of my homeland, far from kinsmen, had to bind with fetters my inmost thoughts after I covered my gold-friend in earth's darkness years ago and, abject and winter-sad, I went away over the frozen waves; sad for want of a hall, I sought a giver of treasure wherever I might find, far or near, one in a mead-hall who might know about my people or be willing to comfort me, a friendless man, to entertain me with joys.—He knows who finds out by experience how cruel is sorrow as a companion for a man who has no beloved protectors.

(lines 19–31)

The central image of *The Wanderer* uses the legal concept of loyalty. A lord is "gold-friend" and "giver of treasure." A man without a lord is "friendless," here as in I Cnut 5.2a and II Cnut 35. The social values of mead halls, joyous entertainment, companionship are evoked. The picture is a perfect one of the man without identity, without a meaningful place and role in human society. It is so evocative of alienation and so seemingly autobiographical that readers have asked more of it than it is willing to reveal. Why did the retainer outlive his lord? Was he unwilling to fulfill the obligation to fight to the death after his lord had been felled? If his lord died of old age in bed, why was the retainer not kept on by the heir? Is the wanderer guilty of some breach of the obligations of loyalty, and does his bad reputation and disgrace somehow go before him to the halls where, fruitlessly, he seeks a new gold-friend? But these are questions the poet neither wants nor needs to answer; for the poet is not the persona of the poem, and the exact experience of the persona is not the point of the poem.

The "finest" Old English poetic diction, E. G. Stanley has argued, "is that in which a state of mind or moral concept evokes in the poem the description of a natural phenomenon, associated by the Anglo-Saxons with that mood or moral concept; . . . it is the thought that gives the flower, not the flower that gives the thought." We must look, in other words, to the context in which the friendless wanderer and the other images appear in the poem. In the first five lines of *The Wanderer*, the speaker identifies himself as a "solitary" who has had to travel "paths of exile" over the "frost-cold sea." He is, further, in search of God's grace or mercy; and he concludes his statement with the chilling observation, *Wyrd biþ full aræd*—a simple statement which is virtually untranslatable but means something like, "What happens is beyond the control of man," or, "Fate is absolutely inflexible."

Two images or conventional rhetorical topics in these lines require attention. The first is winter or, more accurately, the sea in winter. Winter images in Old English poetry usually denote not simply cold but also misery; and a Latin winter topic, which often plays upon the notion that nature in winter is put in bondage by fetters of ice, is now recognized as one which was frequently used by the Old English poets. The winter theme is reinforced again and again later in the poem.

The second image is that of the solitary, sad man who treads the paths of exile. It, too, is a commonplace in Old English literature. The laws and the fate of the sons of Odda in *The Battle of Maldon* sufficiently indicate its secular possibilities, but it has, as well, several kinds of ramifications as a religious image. Exile or peregrination was, for one thing, an image for the monastic life in which one abandoned the ways of the world and became a stranger to them. If this is among the overtones of the poem, at least part of its reference is to the contemplative life— or the contemplative view of life—and one might recall the Cynewulfian and Gregorian simile which compares man's life to a ship, tossed on the hostile sea and trying to make a harbor, which signifies either the way of contemplation or the Kingdom of Heaven or both. But the topic of exile in Christian literature has also a wider and more common meaning. Since the loss of Paradise man has been in exile, for he has lost his true native land and lives in an alien world seeking to return to his proper home with God.

Since *The Wanderer* begins with a reference to the quest for grace, one suspects that the latter implications of exile are its subject. Man's life is an exile in a hostile environment over which he has no control. At the outset the poet has brought together traditional topics or images which state a basic proposition (that human existence is characterized by alienation) and reinforce the proposition by appeal to several kinds of experience. The poem is not autobiographical, because it is immediately set in the context of the lot of mankind in general. All men are exiles in search of mercy. The picture of lines 19–26 both expands the basic topics of the poem and illustrates the initial proposition by appealing to common experience.

But there is another aspect of the context of the experience of the wanderer. He speaks next (after the narrator's comment in lines 6–7) of solitude and agony in the early morning, but argues against the impulse to lament one's woes. A man should keep his troubles to himself; complaint does not change what happens. The sentiments recall commonplace advice to endure hardship with stoic silence, and their effect is to heighten the sense of isolation.

At this point the picture of the lordless man in search of patronage is introduced. No more need be said about it at this juncture, except that *eðel* ("homeland," line 20) may, in the light of the implications of life as exile which are set out at the opening of the poem, mean the heavenly as well as the earthly home. But one has the impression—especially in the light of lines 22–23a—that the image may be restricted to worldly lordlessness. At any rate, the entire first passage of the poem is crowned by lines 34–57 in which the poet shifts to the third person. Yearning for a lord and companions, the lonely exile first remembers and then dreams of the friends and the protector who are lost and, finally, in hallucination, imagines he is with his friends again. But the reality of aloneness breaks through once more. Sorrow, as always, returns to the exile.

At line 58, there begins a second movement of the poem, which has sometimes been attributed to a second speaker. It broadens and generalizes the themes of lines 1–57. Its theme is that life in the world *is* transitory and unstable, as common experience proves; and, to develop this thought, the poet gives a virtuoso's display of the traditional devices for the exposition of the notion.

Lines 58–72 return to the theme of meeting hardship with resigned silence. Death and change of fortune alone are enough to make any man desperately sorrowful. But the very fact of death demonstrates the further fact that the world is aging. Wisdom comes with age, and a man must restrain his despair until he has achieved understanding. To a great extent the effectiveness of these lines depends upon the development of the statement that wisdom is a function of age in connection with the observation that the world is "drooping and falling." For here (and more clearly in *The Searfarer*) is the notion that the cosmos is aging and nearing the end of its existence. Against that notion is set the idea that the history of a man's existence is comparable with the history of the cosmos. A young man is strong but not yet wise, so he must restrain himself from speaking about human hardship until he has achieved wisdom.

The wise man, according to lines 73–84, perceives the transitoriness of the world. He observes ruined dwellings and recognizes that the men who lived there have died, probably violently. The double theme of the transitoriness of the world and of men is thus continued, reinforced by the ruin topic; and the ways a warrior can die are enumerated. The wise man, contemplating such evidences as ruined walls, which seem the work of the giants of the golden age, asks where the men, their horses, their treasures, and their joys have gone. His words, cast in the rhetorical *ubi sunt* framework (lines 92–93) employ a favorite device for dramatizing the theme of mutability. Time has taken its toll, and now there are only walls, buffeted by winter's storms, bound by frost. Life is transitory.

The narrator concludes after the wise one has finished speaking (lines 111–115). The good man keeps his pledges and guards his tongue. It will turn out well for the man who seeks God's mercy, for the only true stability is in heaven. The eschatological point to which all the images of the poem have been implicitly directed is not explicitly stated before the last lines. Thus, unless the reader has been following the overtones or conventional meanings of the images and rhetoric of the poem, he may have forgotten that it begins with a reference to the quest for mercy or grace and may then be surprised when that concept arises again. But if the reader has been in tune, so to speak, with the vibrations of the deeply traditional devices around which the poem is developed, he must have been at least intuitively aware throughout that against the instability of the world, its hardship and aloneness, there stands the stability or dependability of God, whose heaven is the homeland mankind in exile seeks to gain. Grace is the envelope which encloses the poem.

There has been much disagreement as to how to define the

genre of *The Wanderer*. Some have argued that it is to be taken as allegorical, others as elegiac, and still others as fitting the classical literary pattern of consolation. Clearly it verges on all three; and—unless a radically new and conclusive approach is forthcoming—a given reader will decide according to the manner in which he weighs the cumulative effect of the assemblage of images in the poem.

It does seem clear, however, that any appreciation of *The Wanderer* must take account of the fact that the poem is a tissue of traditional images and rhetorical devices—by no means all of which have been catalogued in the reading above. To say this, given the cult of originality in modern literature, may seem heretical to the novice reader of earlier English literature. If, however, one remembers the deep respect of early medieval men for tradition, their approach to education, and their reverence for the wise men of past ages, the recognition that almost everything written has its roots in the past is not surprising. The literature is to be judged not in terms of its originality but in terms of the skill with which the forms and ideas of tradition are handled. If the writer, be he homilist or poet, is successful, the work will appear to be fresh and will speak with authenticity and authority to our own experience. It will not do so in spite of its traditionalism but because the writer is skillful. *Crafty* in modern English has come to mean skillfulness employed to deceive others, guile, cunning. *Cræftig* in Old English denotes skillfulness, ingenuity, learnedness. The *cræftig* writer is one who has learned to use all the resources of the traditions of literature.

The craft of the poet of *The Wanderer* still speaks to our experience of alienation, loneliness, the unpredictability of fortune, the hostility, violence, and senselessness of much that happens to us. It does so in large part because the poet was concerned not so much with his own, individual experiences as because he spoke of human experience. It does so, too, in spite of the fact that few modern readers can follow the poet to his conclusion that our proper homeland is not of this world. It is his *cræft* that makes this poet's work something more than a curious, early document in a vernacular language.

One suspects that the tenth-century reader who selected *The Wanderer* for inclusion in his anthology, the Exeter Book, responded to the poem basically as we do: it speaks with authority to human experience. The reader of a millennium ago, however, probably recognized as well the nature of the poet's craft. He doubtless recognized more than we can ever learn; but by attempting so far as possible to put ourselves into the situation of that earlier reader we can at least come closer to an understanding of how the poem achieved the greatness which renders it still effective after a thousand years. Indeed, we may find ourselves astounded by its sophistication and the skill of its author.

Appendices

APPENDIX I:
SOME NOTES ON ANGLO-SAXON ART AND ARCHITECTURE

No one can be fully cognizant of the scope, richness, and sophistication of the society of the Anglo-Saxons before he is acquainted with the physical and artistic remains of their culture.
Three kinds of sources for this study are available: 1) the churches
which survive throughout England in testimony to the architectural
skill and resources available to ecclesiastical builders; 2) lesser
artifacts, now mostly preserved in British museums, which range
from grave goods to ivories, coins, jewelery, embroidery and
sculpture (which itself ranges from scraps of architectural detail
to monumental crosses); 3) illuminated manuscripts which, in addition to being literary sources, are our best sources of information about the painting of the Anglo-Saxon age.

What follows is the most minimal introduction for students of
literature to two aspects of Anglo-Saxon art which are often
overlooked. I have emphasized here, as elsewhere in this book,
work of the later period and have restricted myself to some
chief architectural monuments and to a previously unpublished
portion of a manuscript with narrative illustrations. It is assumed
that the reader is acquainted or will soon become acquainted
with important earlier artistic achievements such as the Sutton
Hoo objects, the Franks casket, the Lindisfarne Gospels, the Ruth-
well and Bewcastle crosses.

A. ARCHITECTURE

It is surprising how much remains, although it is also disap-
pointing that most of the architectural remains of the Anglo-

Plate 3.
Brixworth Church: The Towers.

Saxon period have been so tampered with that great feats of imagination and scholarship are needed if one is to conceive the original state of the buildings.

Frequently it is said that the Anglo-Saxons were able to build in stone only when they had Roman-quarried stone available. It is true that Roman stone constructions were often robbed by Saxon church-builders. Often one can see the Roman stone-finishing marks (and sometimes even inscriptions) on stones which were incorporated in church buildings. Elsewhere, Saxon builders frequently used Roman stone for the quoining or corner structure of their buildings and used smaller stone (called "rubble") for the main portions of the walls. Roman brick was often used both for walls and for arch-work (Plates 3, 4). Traces of the robbed Roman materials *(spolia)* and of the rubble walls were probably covered by stucco or plaster, as in the plastered wall of a church discovered below the Norman castle of Winchester in 1969. These devices, however, should not be taken as low indices of the skill of the builders. Even in Rome classical walls were robbed by church builders, and in England the fabric of many churches (for example, the Old Minster at Winchester) was used by the Normans in their new buildings. The same fate was met by medieval monasteries after the dissolution in the sixteenth century, when they were used as quarries for public and private building projects. It is probably correct to believe, with writers from Bede to Wulfstan the Cantor, that Anglo-Saxon architecture and decoration from the seventh century to the eleventh were unrivaled in Europe for richness and sophistication. Geographical factors, such as the local availability of stone, had more influence on techniques of construction than limitations of skill.

The earlier churches tend to be fairly small, as was also the case on the Continent in the Merovingian period, but where there is literary evidence (as for the churches built at Monkwearmouth and Jarrow by Benedict Biscop, and at Hexham and elsewhere by Wilfrid) it is known that they were richly decorated with sculpture and painting (not to mention the visual effects of their rich collections of liturgical vestments and vessels) and that craftsmen were brought from the Continent to supervise the work.

The two most complete surviving churches are at Wing (Buckinghamshire) and Brixworth (Northamptonshire). Both were prob-

PLATE 4.
  Brixworth Church: Note the use of Roman brick for the arches.

PLATE 5.
The Crypt at Wing.

ably basilical in plan: that is, they had arcaded naves lit by clerestory windows and either aisles or a series of aisle chapels (*porticus*) to the north and south. Brixworth had a choir separated from the nave by a triple Romanesque archway (now replaced by a single Gothic arch) and perhaps topped with a tower. The polygonal apses of both churches, which were probably originally not the setting of the altars but of the presbyteria, are raised and set off by archways; and to the sides of the chancel arches, there are traces of doorways leading to crypts, which probably enclosed shrines for relics. The crypt of the church at Wing (Plate 5) can still be seen, now exposed beneath the chancel and deprived of the structures which enclosed it and of the entrances from the church nave; vaguely similar crypts from St. Wilfrid's churches at Ripon and Hexham (both of Roman stone covered with plaster and fitted with ingenious lamp-wells) have been incorporated in later structures. The tower at Wing has been replaced, but at Brixworth the later square tower (Plate 3) incorporates an original two-storied porch or westwork which—to judge from remains of archways visible in the west wall of the nave—may have contained a chapel and/or an opening to a gallery or raised chapel at the west end of the church. Arches at Wing suggest that some sort of second-story gallery may also have been a feature of that church. Excavation at Brixworth has shown that the central chamber of the west-end tower structure had flanking chambers.

The earlier portions of the structure at Brixworth, which has had more attention recently than Wing, have been variously dated. It is conceivable that the structure incorporates seventh-century work, but a recent study argues that the earliest fabric is from the latter half of the eighth century. Whatever the date, one is impressed by the sophistication of the builders (despite the fact that much of their building material was Roman) and by their indebtedness to significant models from remote parts of the Christian world.

There is also evidence of a great deal of reconstruction in the late Saxon period. At Brixworth, for example, the two-storied porch was raised to serve as a bell tower. Although one recent student of the church has suggested that this addition was made in the early part of the ninth century and did not serve as a bell tower, other evidence suggests that high towers were introduced for the purpose of housing belfries after the example of Cluny. If this is correct, the upward extension of the western porches of Anglo-Saxon churches is probably to be associated with the tenth-century monastic reform and is an example of the influence of contemporary Continental styles. In the interior west wall at Brixworth, an earlier archway window or door to the porch was blocked and a new, triple-arched window with unusual baluster shafts was substituted at a slightly higher level. The original contours of the top of the square tower are unclear since a later upper story was added when the nave walls received their present finish work. At the same time as the porch of Brixworth was made into a tower, a round stair-tower was added farther to the west. It is unique among the surviving Saxon towers, and the stone, spiral staircase which it encloses is a truly remarkable feat. The original additions to the porch must have extended the square tower to at least the height of the round, stairway turret.

Unfortunately, most of the grander examples of late Anglo-Saxon

PLATE 6.
Foundation of Abbot Wulfric's Rotunda, Canterbury.

building are lost to all but occasional archaeological examination because they were at important sites which were rebuilt and transformed by the Norman bishops and abbots. At Canterbury, however, the exposed foundations of the monastery founded by St. Augustine and later renamed in his honor, show an elaborate sequence of building which included graves for the early archbishops and abbots in the porch or *porticus* of St. Gregory on the north and an equivalent shrine for the kings of Kent to the south. A series of churches built on the same east-west axis was gradually incorporated into a single great abbey church. Abbot Wulfric in the eleventh century undertook to unite the original church of Sts. Peter and Paul with the easterly St. Mary's by means of a rotunda or central tower, of which the crypt and foundations remain (Plate 6). The work, modeled on Continental churches, was never finished, although the Norman church did incorporate both of the Saxon buildings which Wulfric had sought to unite.

A third church, St. Pancras, was some distance farther to the east and was never incorporated in the complex.

At Winchester, the seat of Alfred the Great and his heirs, recent archaeological work has revealed the outlines of an impressive complex of royal and ecclesiastical buildings. The site of Winchester has been occupied since before the Roman occupation. Under the Romans, *Venta Belgarum* was fortified on approximately the same perimeters as the medieval city. Much of its street grid and the probable location of the forum (near the site of the Anglo-Saxon minsters and the Norman cathedral) have been discovered in the course of the recent excavations. The evidence indicates that Winchester continued to be occupied in the early Saxon period, although the West-Saxon settlement can scarcely be said to have continued the ordered, urban life of the Roman period. The earliest Saxon buildings seem, for example, to have been erected on the Roman streets, which afforded readymade foundations, flooring, and drainage; therefore the medieval high street was only one street-width removed from the main Roman east-west street because it gave access to the main city gates, although the other medieval streets bear no relation to the Roman plan. The rebuilding of the fortifications at Winchester by Alfred was essentially a restoration of the Roman walls, and from that time onward the town, as the center of the kingdom of the West Saxons, was a chief center of Anglo-Saxon culture.

It has long been known from the literary evidence that important and impressive buildings were erected at Winchester, but excavation has finally revealed just how important and impressive these structures were. The two chief churches, the Old and New Minsters, had both been destroyed by the Normans to make way for their cathedral and its precincts; but the foundations of the Old Minster have now been completely excavated, and enough work has been done to show that a similar job can be undertaken on the site of the adjacent New Minster.

The original church on the Old Minster site was a structure not quite one hundred feet long, including the sanctuary to the east, with *porticus* on the north and south sides of the eastern end of the main or nave structure. Presumably, this was the church built by King Kenwalh in the middle of the seventh century. More than fifty feet west of the church was a smaller,

square structure, identified as the tower of St. Martin; and between these two buildings on the same axis were the grave of
St. Swithun and a cross. Two extensive series of enlargements
and rebuilding were undertaken in the tenth century by the
party of the monastic reform. First, during the period 971–980
in the episcopate of Æthelwold, the body of Swithun was translated from its outdoor resting place, and the area between the
tower and the church was enclosed and incorporated in the Minster. This work was dedicated in 980. Later under Æthelwold's
successor Alphege, the eastern end of the church was extended
by means of the addition of a new apse and crypt, and other
elaborations were made to the body of the church. The evidence
suggests that the main shrine of St. Swithun was restored to the
site of the original grave, which must have continued to be important as the scene of numerous miracles. The overall length of
the final structure was more than three hundred feet.

What the building looked like is more difficult to say, since
no superstructure survives. (The evidence from trenches for the
plan of the foundations is itself extremely difficult to interpret.)
The literary evidence, in particular a poetic account in Latin of
the life and miracles of St. Swithun which is attributed to Wulfstan the Cantor, suggests that it was a splendid edifice with an
elaborate west work and towers which may have resembled such
important Continental churches as St. Riquier and Corvey. At
any rate, the foundations and such artifacts as the relief carving
mentioned above in the first section of Chapter II (Plate 1) and
a lovely fragment of a large wall-painting on stone are sufficient
warrant that the builders of the churches of Winchester in the
tenth century had the skill and wealth to erect buildings which
could rival in grandeur the most important European edifices of
the same period. With the Old Minster and the equally impressive
New Minster (which had been planned by Alfred, built by his
son, Edward the Elder, and furnished with a splendid tower in
the tenth century), the numerous other churches, and the royal
residence, Winchester must have been an imposing royal and
ecclesiastical center.

Anglo-Saxon architecture was not only impressive but also comparable to building on the Continent. The architectural history
of the age shows that, from the period of Alfred and the mo-

nastic reform to the coming of the Normans, the achievements of builders complemented those of leaders of church and state and of writers.

B. NARRATIVE PAINTING

Winchester was also an important center for book production and painting in the tenth and eleventh centuries and, because of its preeminence in this regard, lent its name in the term "Winchester school" to the mainstream of painting in the late Anglo-Saxon period. There are a number of important recent studies of the art of the Winchester school, and there is no need to dwell here upon its characteristics and achievements. An outgrowth of Carolingian traditions of painting, it became the national style from the middle of the tenth century through (and beyond) the Conquest. (Hence the term "school" is actually a misnomer.) Some of the great works of the Winchester school, like the Benedictional of St. Æthelwold (British Museum, Additional MS. 59598) are richly colored and lavish in their use of gold. Others are illuminated with simple and effective line drawings.

One fact of utmost importance for the understanding and appreciation of the Winchester manuscript paintings is the conventional nature of their subject matter. Like the biblical commentator, the illustrator of the Early Middle Ages restricted himself to traditional themes and to iconographic conventions for the depiction of the themes. Occasionally, it has been possible to trace traditions of illustrations. Thus, for example, it has been shown that the illustrations of the Utrecht Psalter, which was made in Rheims in the first half of the ninth century and was at St. Augustine's Abbey in Canterbury in the late-Saxon period, exercised a very strong influence on Anglo-Saxon Psalter illustration. Its paintings, which are based on the exegetical tradition for the interpretation of the Psalms and on a much earlier iconographic tradition, were copied or adapted for several other Psalters in England; and the artists who illustrated the so-called Cædmon manuscript (Oxford, Bodleian MS. Junius 11) were also strongly influenced by the style and manner of the Psalter painters.

One of the most important examples of narrative biblical illustration from the Winchester school is a manuscript of Ælfric's

PLATE 7.
Noah's Embarkation.

paraphrase of the Hexateuch (British Museum, Cotton MS.
Claudius, B. IV), which was executed at Canterbury about 1050.
It contains over four hundred illustrations, some of which are
line drawings, although the majority are colored. Towards the
end of the book, some of the pictures are unfinished or lacking,
and elsewhere the pictures seem occasionally to have been drawn
before the text was transcribed. Thus a study of the manuscript
affords a striking introduction to the processes of book writing and
illumination. It has been suggested that a tenth-century copy of
an early Christian manuscript of the Old Testament was used by
the illustrators for their iconographic authority; and it is also
maintained that the narrative conventions of the book are not
unlike those of the artists of the Bayeux tapestry.

In an effort to give some sense of the narrative progression of the illuminations and their relationship to the written text, folios 14–18 of Cotton MS. Claudius, B. IV, are reproduced here as Plates 7–11, greatly reduced from the original book, the folios of which measure approximately 12 × 18 inches. These folios contain Ælfric's version of the story of Noah in Genesis, chaps. 6–9 (folio 13^v, which depicts the call of Noah and the building of the ark, has been omitted). The drawings, colored in pastels, are typical of Winchester school illumination. The treatment of drapery is characteristically agitated and contributes to a sense of movement. At least once (lower picture on folio 14, Plate 7), the frequent impatience of the Winchester artists with their own borders is manifested, as the figure-head of the ark pushes past the frame of the picture into the margin of the page. At moments, particularly in the highly stylized treatment of Noah's vine on folio 17 (Plate 10b), the painting betrays what has been considered an influence of "Viking taste," which was not uncommon in the middle of the eleventh century.

Folio 14 (Plate 7) contains only three lines of Ælfric's text (Genesis 7: middle of 7–8), although two twelfth-century annotators have added notes: the first, at the very top of the page, names Noah's and his sons' wives; the second has added Latin comments between and below the pictures. In the upper illustration, God and Noah speak. In the lower, the loaded ark is depicted: it has an elaborate animal figurehead; its three decks (arranged in a manner reminiscent of some early medieval towers) hold, respectively, animals, fowls, and human beings.

Folios 14^v–15 (Plate 8) reproduce the text of Genesis 7:10–8:9 and have Latin annotations below the illustrations. Both pictures are of the ark, closed during the flood, but the drawing on folio 15 shows the raven which Noah first sent from the ark. There is no effort in the first picture to depict the water and none in the second to show Mount Ararat. This is probably because the artist omits details of background when they are not integral to his narrative purposes, but it may also be because he is more concerned to emphasize the common observation of the exegetical tradition that the ark is the type of the church, the vehicle of salvation. The details of the hardware of the door and window of the ark and of some of the planking of the topmost deck are omitted in the second drawing.

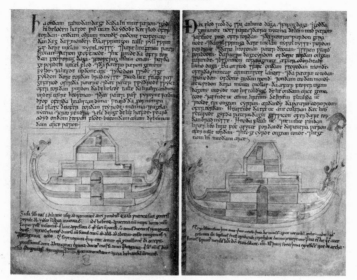

PLATE 8.
Noah: a) During the Flood; b) The Raven.

One interesting feature of the depiction of the raven on folio 15 is that it sits on a head which is apparently impaled on a pike and seems to be picking at one of the eyes of the head. Thus the scene is reminiscent of the fact that the raven is a bird of prey and one of the usual beasts of battle in Old English poetry. The exegetes were interested in the raven and puzzled over its meaning. They had developed a number of explanations. Bede, noting that in the Vulgate it is said that the raven went out and did not return until the waters had dried up, makes it the type of the Christian who elects to live in the world in contrast to the dove, which he takes as the contemplative. But the artist must have in mind some variant of the tradition employed by the author of *Genesis A:*

> Noah considered that in need, if he [the raven] should not find land on the journey, he would seek him over the wide water in the vessel. But his expectation was in error, for the enemy [?] lit upon a floating corpse; the dark-feathered one would not seek him.
>
> (lines 1443–1448)

The head of the raven's prey must be impaled in the picture either because the painter does not want to depict the water or because he is working on some other variant of the tradition. At any rate, the picture stresses the fact that those outside the ark (which is the type of the church) have been judged by God.

PLATE 9.
    Noah's Disembarkation.

PLATE 10.
    Noah: a) Covenant and Rainbow; b) The Vineyard.

The illustration on folio 15ᵛ (Plate 9) depicts simultaneously (in a clockwise movement) four moments described in the text of Genesis 8:10–18: the return of the dove with the olive twig, the removal of the hatch of the ark (despite its door and window), God's command to go forth from the ark, and the disembarkation. Stylized vegetation and terrain are provided as footing for the animals and Noah's family as they leave the ark. The facing page is entirely devoted to text (Genesis 8:30–9:17). Perhaps Noah's sacrifice was considered an unedifying subject, and the terms of the covenant, once the scribe had gone on, took too much space to allow for its depiction on this side of the leaf.

Folio 16ᵛ (Plate 10a) has the text of only the last part of Genesis 9:17 and of verses 18–19. The rest of the page is devoted to a magnificent depiction of the giving of the covenant and of the rainbow. Noah kneels barefoot before God, who holds (as in his earlier appearances) a tablet of laws; his family (one daughter-

PLATE 11.
  Noah: a) Noah's Drunkenness; b) Punishment of Ham and Death of Noah.

in-law is missing) stand by in an attitude of wonder. Annotators have, unfortunately, filled the originally empty space within the rainbow with notes concerning its significance.

The last three pages devoted to the Noah story in the manuscript depict in remarkable detail the later history of Noah, now usually all-but-forgotten and omitted elsewhere by Ælfric. Noah is shown tending his vineyard in the upper picture of folio 17 (Plate 10b). Below, he and members of the family harvest the grapes and press them for wine—a subject on which the biblical text does not dwell. On the reverse of 17 (Plate 11a), the first illumination is a multiple scene which must be read clockwise: above at the left, Noah is seen drinking; on the right, he sleeps naked in his tent and Ham spies on him; at the bottom left, Ham tells Shem and Japheth. The scenes are distinguished by the frame on the left, which suggests a two-story house, and by the stylized tent into which Ham peeks as he leans across the frame. Ham's report to his brothers is made distinct both by the frame and by the fact that, as he reports, Ham turns his back on the picture of himself spying on Noah. The latter device was typical of such narrative picture series as the Bayeux Tapestry.

The second illumination on folio 17^v shows Shem and Japheth covering their father, taking care not to see his nakedness; Ham looks on. At the top of folio 18, Noah awakens and punishes Ham by making him a slave to his brothers. The biblical writer has said shortly before that Ham is the father of Canaan, and this scene was intended to explain that the subjection of the Canaanites to the Israelites was both deserved and a part of the divine scheme of things. The last picture shows Shem and Japheth, surrounded by mourners, wrapping their dead father's body in a shroud for burial.

The effect of the whole series is of loving and detailed narrative which reinforces the text and comments upon it but might almost stand alone. Both Ælfric, who translated the Latin text, and the artist are aware of the larger meanings of the tale they are telling as those meanings had been spelled out in the exegetical tradition, and some hints of this awareness have found expression. But primarily both are concerned to communicate economically the essence of the historical or literal meaning of the tale they found in the Latin version of Genesis.

The narrative style of the painters of the Hexateuch is interesting. They clearly wanted to tell the Noah story in some detail, omitting—with the exception of Noah's sacrifice—no significant incident. Thus the series can be regarded as a whole (and the same can be said of the entire codex). As we have already said, individual pictures (notably folio 15.ᵛ[Plate 9] and the upper picture of 17ᵛ [Plate 11a]), sometimes depict a series of events in clockwise movement. Yet each page is also an artistic whole, a scene one contemplates momentarily on its own. Pairs of pages, notably folios 14ᵛ–15 (Plate 8) and 17ᵛ–18 (Plate 11a and b), are also clearly intended to be read as unified compositions. Furthermore, variations in the treatment of subject, frame, and color divide the ark story from the later portions of the history of Noah, making the two stories about Noah self-sufficient. The treatment is, I think, analogous to the narrative techniques of the poets: consider, for example, the relationship between individual events and scenes and of the two parts in *Beowulf*.

APPENDIX II:

BIBLIOGRAPHICAL NOTES

These notes follow approximately the order in which materials are considered in the text of this book, except that section I is as much devoted to general bibliographical matters as to documentation of Chapter I and section V is related to Appendix I. With the exception of Chapter IV, the materials of which are rather varied, it has not seemed necessary to reflect textual subdivisions in the notes.

I. GENERAL AND INTRODUCTORY

The two best recent, general studies of OE literature are S. B. Greenfield, *A History of Old English Literature* (1965), and C. L. Wrenn, *A Study of Old English Literature* (1967).

The standard collection of the poetic corpus is G. P. Krapp and E. V. K. Dobbie, eds., *Anglo-Saxon Poetic Records*, 6 vols. (1931–1953) [hereafter, *ASPR*]. I frequently refer to other editions, particularly those in Methuen's OE Library and J. C. Pope, ed., *Seven Old English Poems* (1966). Many texts are also published by the Early English Text Society (EETS). On manuscripts, consult N. R. Ker, *Catalogue of Manuscripts containing Anglo-Saxon* (1957). Many mss. are now being published in the superb series, *Early English Manuscripts in Facsimile*.

For bibliography, see Greenfield in D. M. Zesmer, *Guide to English Literature from Beowulf through Chaucer* . . . (1961). To Greenfield's Sec. B on bibliography, add F. C. Robinson, *Old English Literature: A Select Bibliography* (1970), and W. Bonser, *An Anglo-Saxon and Celtic Bibliography* (1957)—the latter for fields other than literature. An annual bibliography compiled by Robinson and commentary thereon appear in *Old English Newsletter*. Cambridge University Press has announced a new annual, *Anglo-Saxon England* (from 1972), which will also print bibliography.

Recent studies of medieval literature in several languages are listed in J. H. Fisher, ed., *The Medieval Literature of Western Europe* (1965). For general surveys of early Germanic literature, see H. M. Chadwick, *The Heroic Age* (1912) and W. T. H. Jackson, *Medieval Literature: A History and a Guide* (1965).

On early medieval Latin literature, see M. W. L. Laistner, *Thought and Letters in Western Europe* (1957), and W. F. Bolton, *A History of Anglo-Latin Literature* (vol. I, 1967; vol. II to appear). Three great collections of medieval Latin texts should be known to all students of OE: J.-P. Migne, ed., *Patrologia Latina [PL]; Corpus Christianorum,*

Series Latina [*CCL*] (in progress, slowly replacing *PL*); *Monumenta Germaniae Historica* [*MGH*] (documents from the Germanic areas).

Among recommended general historical studies are F. Lot, *The End of the Ancient World and the Beginning of the Middle Ages* (trans. 1931), and J. M. Wallace-Hadrill, *The Barbarian West* (2nd ed., 1962). H. Pirenne's thesis is most clearly stated in *Mohammed and Charlemagne* (trans. 1939). The best work on the transition between the Early and High Middle Ages is R. W. Southern, *The Making of the Middle Ages* (1953).

The standard histories of the Anglo-Saxons are F. M. Stenton, *Anglo-Saxon England* (2nd ed., 1947); D. Whitelock, *The Beginnings of English Society* (1952); P. H. Blair, *An Introduction to Anglo-Saxon England* (1956). More recent is D. P. Kirby, *The Making of Early England* (1968). D. Whitelock, ed., *English Historical Documents*, I (1955) [*EHD*, I], is invaluable for texts and introductions.

Recent, useful collections of critical articles on OE literature include J. B. Bessinger, Jr., and S. J. Kahrl, eds., *Essential Articles for the Study of Old English Poetry* (1968); M. Stevens and J. Mandel, eds., *Old English Literature: Twenty-two Analytical Essays* (1968); and L. E. Nicholson, ed., *An Anthology of Beowulf Criticism* (1963).

The essay of R. W. Chambers mentioned in chap. I is *On the Continuity of English Prose from Alfred to More* . . . (EETS, 1932).

II. GERMANIC BACKGROUNDS

Texts and criticism:

For *Deor*, in addition to *ASPR* (III, 178–9) and Pope, 39–40, see K. Malone's ed. (1966). For criticism, see also F. Norman, "Problems of Dating *Deor* and its Allusions," in Bessinger and R. P. Creed, eds., *Franciplegius* (1965); M. W. Bloomfield, "The Form of *Deor*," *PMLA,*" LXXIX (1964), 534–41; Greenfield, *Critical History*, 97, 228–29. Translation (incorporating emendations of Pope and Malone) mine.

On *Widsith*, see *ASPR* (III, 149–53) and the eds. of K. Malone (rev. 1962) and Chambers (1912). Trans. R. K. Gordon, *Anglo-Saxon Poetry* (rev. 1954), 67–70, with occasional inaccuracies.

For *Beowulf*, see F. Klaeber, ed. (3rd with supp., 1950); *ASPR*, IV. See also R. W. Chambers, *Beowulf, An Introduction*, with supp. by C. L. Wrenn (3rd ed., 1959); G. N. Garmonsway et al., *Beowulf and its Analogues* (1968); D. Whitelock, *The Audience of Beowulf* (1951); L. D. Benson, "The Pagan Coloring of *Beowulf*," in R. P. Creed, ed., *Old English Poetry* (1967). Trans. quoted is by K. Crossley-Holland (1968); other recommended translations by B. Raffel (1963) and E. T. Donaldson (1966).

The standard ed. of Bede's *Opera Historica* remains C. Plummer's (1896). A new ed. of the *Ecclesiastical History* with trans. has been made by B. Colgrave and R. A. B. Mynors (1969). Quoted trans. is by L. Sherley-Price (1955). For the *Anglo-Saxon Chronicle* see Plummer's rev. of Earle (1892, 1899); the best trans. are by Whitelock, *EHD*, I (also pub. separately 1961), which I quote, and G. N. Garmonsway (rev. 1954).

De Falsis Diis, the homily of Ælfric to which allusion is made in chap. II, is ed. by J. C. Pope, *Homilies of Ælfric* (1967–68), II, 676–712. The epistles of Alcuin which are mentioned are nos. 20, 124 (*MGH, Epistolarum*, IV).

Studies:

On the problem of paganism, see E. G. Stanley, "The Search for Anglo-Saxon Paganism," *Notes and Queries*, CCIX (1964), 204–209, 242–50, 282–87, 324–31, 455–63; CCX (1965), 9–17, 203–207, 285–93, 322–27.

On genealogies, see K. Sisam, "Anglo-Saxon Royal Genealogies," *Proceedings of the British Academy*, XXXIX (1953), 287–348.

For place-names, consult E. Eckwall, *The Concise Oxford Dictionary of English Place-Names* (4th ed., 1960); K. Cameron, *English Place-Names* (2nd ed., 1963).

The Winchester Sigmund stone is discussed by M. Biddle, "Excavations at Winchester, 1965," *Antiquaries Journal*, XLVI (1966), 329–32.

For the Sutton Hoo treasure, see the British Museum *Handbook* by R. L. S. Bruce-Mitford and C. Green, *Sutton Hoo* (1963).

On the migrations, consult (in addition to historical works cited above) G. Jones, *A History of the Vikings* (1968).

For a good introduction to OE versification, see Pope, *Seven Poems*, pp. 97ff., or his magisterial *The Rhythm of Beowulf* (2nd ed., 1966). The basic work of Sievers (a sample is translated in Bessinger and Kahrl, *Essential Articles*) ought still to be consulted by advanced students.

The standard study of the scop is L. F. Anderson, *The Anglo-Saxon Scop* (1903); it may be supplemented by reference to articles by N. E. Eliason and J. D. A. Ogilvy in *Speculum*, XXXVIII (1963), 267–84 and 603–19, respectively.

On oral poetry, see A. B. Lord, *The Singer of Tales* (1965). The basic application of the work of Parry and Lord to OE poetry is F. P. Magoun, Jr., "The Oral-Formulaic Character of Anglo-Saxon Narrative Poetry," *Speculum*, XXVIII (1953), 446–67. For an important reassessment of the oral-formulaic thesis, see A. C. Watts, *The Lyre and the*

Harp (1969). The quotation of Milman Parry is from *Harvard Studies in Classical Philology*, XLIII (1932), 7–8.

W. P. Lehmann, *The Development of Germanic Verse Form* (1956), surveys the history of poetics in the Germanic languages.

On kennings and *kend heiti*, see A. G. Brodeur, *The Art of Beowulf* (1960), 18ff., 247–53.

On music, see Pope, *Rhythm*, 88–95, and Bessinger, "The Sutton Hoo Harp Replica and Old English Musical Verse," in Creed, ed., *Old English Poetry* (1967), 3–26 (but, since the article was written, the British Museum has reconstructed the instrument as a Germanic lyre).

Tacitus, *Germania*, is easily available. For criticism, see the article of G. Eckholm in *Cambridge Ancient History*, XI (1936), 68–76.

For an interesting mythological approach to *Beowulf*, see A. M. Arent, "The Heroic Pattern," in E. C. Polomé, ed., *Old Norse Literature and Mythology* (1969), 130–199.

Archaeology is surveyed by D. M. Wilson, *The Anglo-Saxons* (1960), and mythology by E. O. G. Turville-Petre, *Myth and Religion of the North* (1964).

On the "lost" literature, see R. M. Wilson, *The Lost Literature of Medieval England* (1952). The Chambers quotation is from his essay of the same title, reprinted in Bessinger and Kahrl, *Essential Articles*.

The Trevor-Roper quotation is from *The Rise of Christian Europe* (1965), 9.

III. Early Medieval Christianity

Texts and criticism:

Regularis Concordia, ed. T. Symons (1953) has text, trans. (quoted here), and valuable introduction.

Bede's *De Schematibus et Tropis,* ed. K. F. von Halm, *Rhetores Latini Minores* (1863), 607–618; quoted trans. by G. H. Tanenhaus in *Quarterly Journal of Speech*, XLVIII (1962), 237–53. For comment, see Bolton, *Anglo-Latin Literature*, I, 159–65.

Bede's *Libri Quatuor in Principium Genesis* is ed. C. W. Jones, *CCL*, CXVIII-A. Trans. mine.

Advent appears in *ASPR*, III; A. S. Cook, *The Christ of Cynewulf* (rev. ed., 1909) [as *Christ*, I]; and two commentaries: J. J. Campbell, *The Advent Lyrics of the Exeter Book* (1959); R. B. Burlin, *The Old English Advent* (1968). Trans. B. Raffel, *Poems from the Old English* (2nd ed., 1964), 69. Among critical essays, consult R. Woolf's review of Campbell *(Medium Ævum,* XXIX [1960], 125–29); E. Burgert, *Dependence of Part I of Cynewulf's Christ upon the Antiphonary*

(1921); J. E. Cross, "The 'Coeternal Beam' in the Old English Advent Poem," *Neophilologus,* XLVII (1964), 72–82; S. B. Greenfield, "The Theme of Spiritual Exile in *Christ I,*" *Philological Quarterly,* XXXII (1953), 321–28.

The anon. *Earliest Life of Gregory the Great* is ed. and trans. by B. Colgrave (1968), from whom I quote. Gregory's *Dialogues* is trans. by O. J. Zimmerman (1959) from the ed. of U. Moricca (1924); other works are in *PL* LXXV–LXXIX, but for the letters see *MGH, Epistolarum,* I–II.

The best ed. of Benedict's *Rule* is by G. Penco (1958); trans. (with uncritical intro.) J. McCann (1952).

Ælfric's *Grammar and Glossary,* ed. J. Zupitza (1880); *Colloquy,* ed. G. N. Garmonsway (2nd ed., 1961); *De Temporibus Anni,* ed., H. Henel (EETS, 1942). Bede's *De Temporum Ratione,* ed. C. W. Jones, *Bedae Opera de Temporibus* (1943).

For Donatus, see H. Keil, ed., *Grammatici Latini,* IV (1864) 355–66 *(Ars Minor),* 367–402 *(Ars Maior);* Priscian, *ibid.,* II–III (1855, 1859).

Cassian's *Collationes* is available in trans. in *Select Library of Nicene and Post-Nicene Fathers,* 2nd Ser., XI. On Cassian, see O. Chadwick, *John Cassian* (2nd ed., 1968).

My trans. from Amalarius, *Liber de Ordine Antiphonarii,* based on the text in *PL,* CV, 1268.

Studies:

On Gregory and Bede, P. Meyvaert's Jarrow Lecture, *Bede and Gregory the Great* (1964) is very informative. There is no full-scale recent study of Gregory, but see the 2 vol. life by F. H. Dudden (1905). On the musical ramifications of the problem of Gregory and liturgics, see W. Apel, *Gregorian Chant* (1958).

The best short history of monasticism is D. Knowles, *Christian Monasticism* (1969); the same author's *Problems in Monastic History* (1963) is the best intro. to the Benedictine problem; and his *The Monastic Order in England* (2nd ed., 1963) is indispensable. On monastic piety and discipline, see C. Butler, *Benedictine Monachism* (2nd ed., 1961). For studies of the last stages of Anglo-Saxon religious history, see R. R. Darlington, "Ecclesiastical Reform . . . ," *English Historical Review,* LI (1936), 385–428; F. Barlow, *The English Church, 1000–1066* (1963).

On the role of logic, see Southern, *Making of the Middle Ages;* and Knowles, *Evolution of Medieval Thought* (1962), esp. 93–106.

The curriculum is described by Laistner, *Thought and Letters;* see also C. S. Baldwin, *Medieval Rhetoric and Poetic* (1928). A very handy book for students is R. A. Lanham, *Handlist of Rhetorical Terms* (1968).

J. J. Campbell, "Knowledge of Rhetorical Figures in Anglo-Saxon England," *JEGP*, LXVI (1967), 1–20, and E. R. Curtius, *European Literature and the Latin Middle Ages* (trans. 1953), are extremely important.

On biblical studies, consult B. Smalley, *The Study of the Bible in the Middle Ages* (2nd ed., 1952), and H. de Lubac, *Exégèse Médiévale*, 2 vols. in 4 parts (1959–1964). See also J. Leclercq, *The Love of Learning and the Desire for God* (trans. 1962).

For typology, consult G. W. H. Lampe and J. K. Woolcombe, *Essays on Typology* (1957). For its classical roots, see R. Pfeiffer, *History of Classical Scholarship* (1968), 237 ff.; E. Auerbach, *Mimesis* (trans. 1953); "Figura," in *Scenes from the Drama of European Literature* (trans. 1959); and *Literary Language and its Public* (trans. 1965). On Augustine's *De Doctrina*, consult F. van der Meer, *Augustine the Bishop* (trans. 1961).

The single most convincing demonstration of the development of a poem according to the dictates of the exegetical method is J. E. Cross, "The Conception of the Old English *Phoenix*," in Creed, ed., *Old English Poetry*, 129–52.

IV. Man and His World in Anglo-Saxon England
A. *MAN AND THE COSMOS*
Texts and criticism:

For *Dream of the Rood*, see Pope, *Seven Old English Poems;* also the ed. of B. Dickins and A. S. C. Ross (rev. 1966).

Boethius, *Philosophiae Consolatio*, is ed. by L. Bieler, *CCL*, XCIV. The quoted trans. is by R. H. Green (1962).

Alfred's Boethius is ed. by W. J. Sedgefield (1899); my trans. based on that text. For commentary, see F. A. Payne, *King Alfred and Boethius* (1968)—from which I differ at some points—and K. Otten, *König Alfreds Boethius* (1964). On Alfred's use of commentaries on Boethius, see B. S. Donaghey, "The Sources of King Alfred's Translation of Boethius . . . ," *Anglia*, LXXXII (1964), 22–57. D. Whitelock surveys Alfred's work in an article in E. G. Stanley, ed., *Continuations and Beginnings* (1966), 67–103.

Byrhtferth's *Manual* is ed. by S. J. Crawford (EETS, 1929).

Studies:

On the ages of the world, see M. Förster, "Die Weltzeitalter bei den Angelsachschen," *Neusprachliche Studien: Festgabe K. Luick* (1925), 183–203. On the aging cosmos, see J. E. Cross, "Aspects of Microcosm and Macrocosm in Old English Literature," *Comparative Literature,* XIV (1962), 1–22.

On the problem of the soul in OE thought, see Gatch, *Death* (1969), 79–92.

E. G. Stanley discusses the history of the interpretation of *wyrd* in *Notes and Queries,* CCX (1965), 285–93, 322–37.

On science, see J. H. G. Grattan and C. J. Singer, *Anglo-Saxon Magic and Medicine* (1952), and C. H. Talbot, *Medicine in Medieval England* (1967), chap. 1. Scientific texts are collected in T. O. Cockayne, *Leechdoms, Wortcunning and Starcraft of Early England* (reprinted with intro. by Singer, 1961).

B. THE ORDERING OF LIFE IN THE WORLD
Texts and criticism:

Wulfstan's *Institutes of Polity* is ed. by K. Jost (1959); trans. mine. On Wulfstan's career, see D. Bethurum in Stanley, *Continuations and Beginnings,* 210–46, and her intro. to *Homilies of Wulfstan* (1957); Whitelock, intro. to *Sermo Lupi ad Anglos* (3rd ed., 1963); Jost. *Wulfstanstudien* (1950). See also Whitelock, "Wulfstan and the Laws of Cnut," *English Historical Review,* LXIII (1948), 433–52, and Bethurum, "Archbishop Wulfstan's Commonplace Book," *PMLA,* LVII (1942), 916–29.

The great ed. of OE laws is by F. Liebermann, *Die Gesetze der Angelsachsen,* 2 vols (1903–1916); generous samples of laws and other legal documents trans. in *EHD,* I (from which I quote). For introduction to laws, see Whitelock, *Beginnings,* 134–54; Blair, *Introduction,* 194–244.

Studies:

A recent, interesting, and controversial survey of the history of Anglo-Saxon law is H. G. Richardson and G. O. Sayles, *Law and Legislation from Æthelberht to Magna Carta* (1966).

Good textbooks of constitutional history *(e.g.,* B. Lyon, *A Constitutional and Legal History of Medieval England* [1960]) are helpful as introductory guides. For Continental legal history, see K. F. Drew, "The Barbarian Kings as Lawgivers and Judges," in R. S. Hoyt, ed., *Life and Thought in the Early Middle Ages* (1967).

C. LOYALTIES IN THE WORLD
Texts and criticism:

My trans. from *Battle of Maldon* is based on the ed. of E. V. Gordon (1960). See also Pope, *Seven Old English Poems.* Critical articles include J. B. Bessinger, *"Maldon* and the *Óláfsdrápa:* an Historical Caveat," *Comparative Literature,* XIV (1962), 23–35; G. Clark, *"The Battle of Maldon:* A Heroic Poem." *Speculum,* XLIII (1968), 52–71; N. F. Blake, *"The Battle of Maldon," Neophilologus,* XLIX (1965), 332–45; J. E. Cross, "Oswald and Byrhtnoth . . . ," *English Studies,* XLVI (1965), 93–109; M. J. Swanton, *"The Battle of Maldon:* a Literary Caveat," *JEGP,* LXVII (1968), 441–50; E. B. Irving, Jr., "The Heroic Style in *The Battle of Maldon,"* *Studies in Philology,* LXVII (1961), 457–67. On the problem of *ofermod,* see also J. R. R. Tolkien, "The Homecoming of Beorhtnoth Beorhthelm's Son," *English Association Essays and Studies,* N.S. VI (1953), 1–24.

Studies:

For the military institutions, see C. W. Hollister, *Anglo-Saxon Military Institutions on the Eve of the Norman Conquest* (1962).

D. THE EXEMPLAR OF LOYALTY AND HEROISM
Texts and criticism:

The *Ascension* of Cynewulf is ed. in *ASPR,* III, by Cook as lines 440–866 of *The Christ of Cynewulf.* The trans. of lines 558–85 is from Pope, "The Lacuna in the Text of Cynewulf's *Ascension* . . . ," in E. B. Atwood and A. A. Hill, eds., *Studies in Language, Literature, and Culture of the Middle Ages and Later* (1969), 210–219; trans. of lines 730b–736a mine; lines 795–807a trans. R. W. V. Elliott, "Cynewulf's Runes in *Christ II* and *Elene," English Studies,* XXXIV (1953), 49–57. For further discussion and bibliog. see Greenfield, *Critical History,* 131–136.

The Gregorian source is *XL Homiliarum in Evangelia Libri Duo,* XXIX. 9–11 *(PL,* LXXVI, 1218–19), and the Bedan is *Hymni et Preces,* VI (In Ascensioni Domini), ed. J. Fraipont *(CCL,* CXXII, 419–23).

Studies:

For biblical and early Christian background of the *descensus,* see J. N. D. Kelly, *Early Christian Creeds* (2nd ed., 1960), 378–88, 398 ff. Southern is also good on the descent: *Making of the Middle Ages,* 234–37.

On runes in general, see Elliott, *Runes* (1959).

On eschatology in OE sermons, see Gatch in *Traditio,* XXI (1965), 117–165.

For the modesty topoi, see Curtius, *European Literature,* 83–85, 515–18.

The problem of the saint as hero and hagiography as a literary genre, which there has not been space to discuss here, is nicely treated by R. Woolf in Stanley, ed., *Continuations and Beginnings,* 36–66.

E. MAN AS ALIEN
Texts and criticism:

My trans. of *Wanderer* is based on the ed. of Pope, *Seven Old English Poems;* see also the ed. by R. F. Leslie (1966). Among the many recent studies of *Wanderer, Seafarer,* and OE literary conventions I have found helpful are E. G. Stanley, "Old English Poetic Diction and the Interpretation of *The Wanderer, The Seafarer* and *The Penitent's Prayer,*" *Anglia,* LXXIII (1955), 413–66; B. K. Martin, "Aspects of Winter in Latin and Old English Poetry," *JEGP,* LXVIII (1969), 375–90; Whitelock, "The Interpretation of *The Seafarer,*" *Early Cultures of North-West Europe (H. M. Chadwick Memorial Studies)* (1950), 259–72; G. V. Smithers, "The Meaning of *The Seafarer* and *The Wanderer,*" *Medium Ævum,* XXVI (1957), 137–53; XXVII (1958), 1–22 99–104; Cross, "On the Genre of *The Wanderer,*" *Neophilologus,* XLV (1961), 63–75; Pope, "Dramatic Voices in *The Wanderer* and *The Seafarer*" in Bessinger and Creed, eds., *Franciplegius,* 164–93; Greenfield, "*Min, Sylf,* and 'Dramatic Voices . . .',*" JEGP,* LXVIII (1969), 212–20; Cross, "Aspects of Microcosm and Macrocosm"; Cross, "On *The Wanderer* Lines 80–84: a Study of a Figure and a Theme," *Vetenskaps-Societetens i Lund Aarsbok* (1958–59), 75–110; Cross, " 'Ubi Sunt' Passages in Old English . . . ," *ibid.* (1956), 23–44.

Supplementary note on The Wanderer

After my discussion of *The Wanderer* was in proof, two important works came to my attention: an edition of the poem by T. P. Dunning and A. J. Bliss (1969), and P. A. M. Clemoes's article, *"Mens absentia cogitans* in *The Seafarer* and *The Wanderer,"* in D. A. Pearsall and R. A. Waldron, eds., *Medieval Literature and Civilization: Studies in Memory of G. N. Garmonsway* (1969), I regret that I could not adjust my text in the light of these contributions. In particular, it should be mentioned that Leslie's notion that lines 51–55a represent an hallucination must be abandoned.

Studies:

For further suggestions on the theme of peregrination, see K. Hughes, "The Changing Theory and Practice of Irish Pilgrimage," *Journal of Ecclesiastical History,* XI (1960), 143–51.

OE rhetorical patterns are discussed by A. C. Bartlett, *The Larger Rhetorical Patterns in Anglo-Saxon Poetry* (1935).

V. ART AND ARCHITECTURE

The standard survey is G. Baldwin Brown, *The Arts in Early England*, 6 vols. in 7 (1915–37). See also D. T. Rice, *English Art, 871–1100* (1952). For architecture, H. M. and Joan Taylor, *Anglo-Saxon Architecture*, 2 vols. (1956). On late ms. illustration, see F. Wormald, *English Drawings of the Tenth and Eleventh Centuries* (1952).

On Brixworth, see E. Gilbert, "Brixworth and the English Basilica," *The Art Bulletin*, XLVII (1956), 1–20.

The literary evidence for Winchester is surveyed by R. N. Quirk, *Archaeological Journal*, CXIV (1957), 28–68 (Old Minster), and *Journal of the British Archaeological Association*, 3rd Ser., XXIV (1961), 16–54 (New Minster). Annual reports on the excavations by M. Biddle are printed in *Archaeological Journal*, CXIX (1962), 159–94, and thereafter in *The Antiquaries Journal*, XLIV (1964), sqq.

On Carolingian monastic buildings, see K. J. Conant, *Carolingian and Romanesque Architecture, 800 to 1200* (1959), esp. 11–29.

A. J. Campbell, "The Richness of the Eadwine Psalter," *Revue de l'Université d'Ottawa*, XXXVIII (1968), 132–43, has good introductory discussion of the Utrecht Psalter tradition.

INDEX
of Ancient and Medieval Authors and Writings

(References to the Bible and to art objects are omitted.)

INDEX